WESTERN
SCHOLARSHIP
and
THE HISTORY OF
PALESTINE

WESTERN SCHOLARSHIP and THE HISTORY OF PALESTINE

Edited by
Michael Prior, CM

MELISENDE
LONDON

First published 1998 by Melisende
An imprint of
Fox Communications and Publications
39 Chelmsford Road
London E18 2PW

General editor: Leonard Harrow
Produced by Fox Communications and Publications, London

ISBN 1 901764 02 8

Cover illustration: detail from *Fountain,* Farah·Jackson

Origination and typesetting by Walden Litho Plates
Printed and bound in England by The Balkerne Press, Colchester

CONTENTS

PREFACE

The Proceedings of the Seventh Jerusalem Day Symposium Amman, October 1996

Dr Subhi Ghosheh

Jerusalem, recognised by UNESCO as one of the most important cities of heritage, must be preserved and maintained in its cultural diversity. Unfortunately, the Israeli authorities conspire to mask and obliterate the city's Arab identity, Islamic and Christian, in defiance of UN Security Council and UNESCO resolutions, and do so with some success. The Palestinians seek the support of the international community to stop this illegal and dangerous alteration of historical realities and of the multicultural nature of the city.

The 'Jerusalem Day' Committee was founded in 1987 as a non-governmental organisation. It is composed of scholars and academics from Palestine and other Arab countries. The main objectives of the committee are to spread an awareness of the authentic Arab Muslim and Christian history of Jerusalem, its archaeological background, its 6000 years of civilisation and culture, its religious monuments, its prominent schools, and of all other aspects of life in this Holy City.

The Committee holds an annual symposium during the first week of October in commemoration of the liberation of Jerusalem by Salahuddin on 2 October 1187. These symposia examine the various aspects of Jerusalem's historical, cultural, archaeological, religious, architectural and social background. The papers are published in Arabic for distribution to universities, academic institutions and scholars throughout the world.

The Seventh Symposium was held in Amman, Jordan, on 5-8 October 1996, under the patronage of HE Taher El-Masri, the former Prime Minister of Jordan. Its theme was 'The Inalienable Arab Rights in Jerusalem'. The programme included the following activities:

A: The Opening Ceremonies

Dr Subhi Ghosheh, Chairman of the Jerusalem Day Committee, welcomed the participants and thanked them for coming from so many different countries for the symposium. He stressed the importance of the participation of scientists, academics, and historians in such symposia, in order to present facts, accurate analysis and proper planning for the preservation of Arab Jerusalem. In his address, Haj Zaki El-Ghoul, a member of the Arab Jerusalem Municipal Council, concentrated on the sufferings of the Arab population of Jerusalem and the need for immediate actions to stop the Judaisation of the city.

HE Mr Taher El-Masri, former Jordanian Prime Minister, called for a unified stand to support Jerusalem, based on the following principles:

— Highlighting both the religious and political importance of the city
— Putting aside any inter-Arab differences concerning the Holy City
— Providing financial support and funding
— Launching an Arab and International media campaign to spread awareness about the illegal Israeli measures being carried out in Jerusalem.

During the opening ceremony, Dr Massoud Abu Baker was presented with the 'Kamel Asali Award for Academic Research', for his work, 'Land Property in Jerusalem District from 1858 to 1918'. The award of 1000 Jordanian Dinars is made annually for the finest academic research on Jerusalem.

The patron of the symposium opened an exhibition of paintings, pictures and books about Jerusalem. There was also a dinner reception in honour of the participants, which included a display of Palestinian costumes, folklore, dances and songs, and a presentation of 'Jerusalem Wedding Ceremonies' by Jerusalem folklore groups.

B: Lectures

The following papers were presented:

Professor Dr Thomas L Thompson,
Professor of Old Testament, University of Copenhagen:

> *Hidden Histories and the Problem of Ethnicity in Palestine,* delivered in English (published herein)

Dr Mahmoud Ahmad A H Al-Zo'bi,
History Department, School of Arts, Damascus University, Syria:

> *Canaanite Arabs: the Builders of Jerusalem and of other Cities of Palestine.* The lecture in Arabic, based on recent archaeological findings, traced the history of Jerusalem back to the Canaanites and their precursors

Professor John B Quigley,
Professor of Law and Political Science, Ohio State University, USA:

> *The Right of Return of Displaced Jerusalemites*, delivered in English (published herein)

Professor Mustafa Ahmed Fouad,
Professor and Head of the International Law Department, and Deputy for Educational and Student Affairs, Tanta University, Egypt:

> *International Protection of Holy Sites.* The lecture in Arabic examined the legal basis that necessitates the formation of an International Agreement to protect the Holy Sites. He insisted that this is a humanitarian issue: 'These sites do not belong to a particular generation. It is the duty of every generation to protect, preserve and maintain them for the next.'

Professor Dr Michael Prior,
Principal Lecturer in Theology and Religious Studies, St Mary's University College, University of Surrey, England; Visiting Professor in Bethlehem University and Scholar-in-Residence in Tantur Ecumenical Institute, Jerusalem:

> *The Moral Problem of the Land Traditions of the Bible,* delivered in English (published herein)

Professor Dr Keith Whitelam,
Professor of Biblical Studies and Head of Department of Religious Studies, University of Stirling, Scotland:

> *Western Scholarship and the Silencing of Palestinian History,* delivered in English (published herein)

Professor Dr Hassan Sayyed Sulaiman,
Head of the Political Science Department, Sana'a University, Yemen:

> *Encroachment on Arab Rights in Jerusalem.* This Lecture in Arabic dealt with one of the most important concerns of the Jerusalem issue, the Israeli aggression on Arab rights in the city. He highlighted the official statements, policies, and measures adopted by the Israelis to Judaise Jerusalem

since 1948, in order to take over the city and turn it into the capital of the Jewish state.

Dr Alai' Al Bitar,
Jerusalem Open University, Jerusalem:

> *Israeli Practices in Violation of Arab Rights in the Fields of Education in Jerusalem, 1967-1996.* In his lecture in Arabic, Dr Bitar presented facts concerning the schools in Jerusalem under Israeli control which impose Israeli-oriented curricula. He highlighted the problems facing Arabs in ensuring the highest academic standards for their schools, and their need for help.

C: Round Table Open Discussion:
Jerusalem and the UN Resolutions

The participants, and subjects discussed, were

Dr Anis Qasem, Editor of *The Palestine Yearbook of International Law* (Moderator)

Dr George Tu'meh, former Syrian Permanent Representative in the UN: *Jerusalem in the UN from 1948-1980*

Dr Hazem Nusseibeh, former Jordanian Minister, and former Jordanian Permanent Representative in the UN: *Arab Inalienable Rights in Jerusalem*

Dr Mohammed El-Farra, former Jordanian Permanent Representative to the UN: *Jerusalem: Where to?*

Professor Dr Mustafa Afifi, Higher Studies Deputy of the Faculty of Law, Tanta University, Egypt: *Arab Rights in Jerusalem. A Historical and Analytical View in Accordance with United Nations Resolutions*

Dr Mohammed Majed Al-Hizmawi, Associate Professor of History, Hebron University Palestine:
Jerusalem in the Light of British and International Committees 1917-1947

Dr Hani El-Hadeethi, Associate Professor, Center of International Studies, Baghdad University, Iraq:
The Inalienable Rights of Arabs in Jerusalem

Dr Ahmad Said Nofal, Professor of Political Science, Yarmouk University, Jordan:
The Conflict between International Decisions, Resolutions and Proposals and Illusory Solutions for Jerusalem

This pan-Arab discussion, which touched on all aspects of the Jerusalem question, and answered questions raised by members of the audience, concluded that there is no solution to the question except through implementation of international decisions, which respect the legitimacy in international law of annulling all the illegal laws and regulations, and the geographic and demographic changes implemented by the Israeli authorities in Jerusalem. The Round Table Discussion stressed that Jerusalem is the key to peace and war, and that the problems surrounding it must be solved in accordance with history, law and justice.

D: Recommendations and Decisions

The Seventh Symposium was concluded with recommendations and decisions which were presented in the final statement, which contains the following points:

a. On the Political Side

1.	Jerusalem is at the heart of the struggle between Arabs and Israelis
2.	Any solution must respect the inalienable Arab rights in Jerusalem and annul all the regulations, rules and changes imposed by the Israelis on Jerusalem

3.　　　International resolutions and decisions to preserve Jerusalem's Arabic, Islamic and Christian identity must be adhered to

4.　　　The international community must help Jerusalemites in their sufferings, and demand the removal of the siege which is continuing to damage Jerusalem's social, economic, cultural, educational and religious institutions.

b. Other Resolutions

5.　　　To request historians to respect the evidence of archaeological research, and to respect the literary forms of the Bible and the contexts of its authors

6.　　　To maximise efforts to form an international committee for the protection of the Holy Sites, and to have an 'International Agreement for the Protection of the Holy Sites'

7.　　　To translate into English and other languages Arabic literature on Jerusalem. This literature seeks to increase the international community's knowledge of the present status of Jerusalem, and to ensure an awareness of the dangers posed by the recent changes in its circumstances, and the atrocities which have been inflicted upon its Arab people.

CONTRIBUTORS

Michael Prior is Principal Lecturer in the Department of Theology and Religious Studies in St Mary's University College, University of Surrey, England, and was Visiting Professor in Bethlehem University, and Scholar-in-Residence in Tantur Ecumenical Institute, Jerusalem (1996-97). He is a graduate in Experimental Physics and Mathematics (Dublin), and in Divinity (Rome). He did postgraduate biblical study in University College (Dublin), the Pontifical Biblical Institute (Rome), King's College (London), and the École Biblique et Archéologique de Jérusalem. He is the author of *Paul the Letter Writer and the Second Letter to Timothy* (Sheffield Academic Press, 1989), *Jesus the Liberator. Nazareth Liberation Theology (Luke 4.16-30)* (Sheffield Academic Press, 1995), *The Bible and Colonialism. A Moral Critique* (Sheffield Academic Press, 1997), and was co-editor of *Christians in the Holy Land* (London: WIFT/Scorpion, 1994).

John Quigley is Professor of Law and Political Science at Ohio State University, Columbus, Ohio, USA. He is a graduate of Harvard Law School, and a member of the bar of the United States Supreme Court and of the bars of Massachusetts and Ohio. He has given testimony in Congress on international questions and at the UN on human rights issues. He has written extensively on legal matters concerning the former USSR and the foreign policy of the USA. He is the author of several books and articles on Israel-Palestine, including *Treatment of Palestinians in Israeli Occupied West Bank and Gaza* (National Lawyers Guild), *International Human Rights Law and Israel's Efforts to Suppress the Palestinian Uprising* (National Lawyers Guild), *Palestine and Israel: A Challenge to Justice* (Duke University Press).

Thomas L Thompson is a graduate of Duquesne University, Pittsburgh, and did postgraduate research in the Ancient Near East and Biblical Studies in Oxford, Tübingen, and Temple University in Philadelphia. Since 1993 he is Professor of Old Testament in the University of Copenhagen, Denmark. Earlier he taught at the Universities of Dayton, Detroit, Lawrence, and Marquette in the USA, and in the *École Biblique* in Jerusalem. He has published widely on topics relating to the Bible, and the history, geography and archaeology of Palestine. His books include *The Historicity of the Pentateuchal Narratives. The Quest for the Historical Abraham* (Berlin/New York: de Gruyter, 1974), *The Settlement of Sinai and the Negev in the Bronze Age* (Wiesbaden, 1975), *The Settlement of Palestine in the Bronze Age* (Wiesbaden, 1979), *The Origin Tradition of Ancient Israel. 1. The Literary Formation of Genesis and Exodus 1-23* (Sheffield: JSOT Press, 1987), *Toponymie Palestinienne. Plaine de St Jean d'Acre et Corridor de Jérusalem* (Louvain-la-Neuve: Université Catholique de Louvain, Institut Orientaliste, with F J Gonçalves and J M van Cangh. 1988), and *Early History of the Israelite People from the Written and Archaeological Sources* (Leiden: Brill, 1992).

Keith W Whitelam is Professor of Religious Studies and Head of the Department of Religious Studies at the University of Stirling, Scotland. He is a graduate in Theology from the University of Manchester where he also completed his postgraduate research. He has written extensively on ancient Israelite and Palestinian history including *The Just King: Monarchical Judicial Authority in Ancient Israel* (Sheffield: JSOT Press, 1979) and *The Emergence of Early Israel in Historical Perspective* (co-author with Robert B Coote; Sheffield: Almond Press, 1987). His most recent book is *The Invention of Ancient Israel: the Silencing of Palestinian History* (London: Routledge, 1996).

INTRODUCTION

Michael Prior

lthough the four papers which follow examine the situation in Israel-Palestine from different perspectives, there is a thematic coherence which reflects a common concern, one which can be described broadly as a passion for historical truth, and for contemporary justice and legality. Three deal with the controlling role of the narrative of the Bible in discussions about the region. Although the focus is distinctive in each case, the three authors insist that the biblical narratives must be examined in terms both of their literary forms and the circumstances of their composition. Two are particularly sensitive to the distortion of the real past which results from refracting the ancient documents through the lenses of nineteenth- and twentieth-century European concepts of nation and state, while the third concentrates on the moral burden of the land traditions of the Bible, which appear to legitimise and even mandate what our generation would regard as crimes against humanity. The final paper also situates an aspect of the contemporary Israel-Palestine conflict in the wider context of international law and conventions on human rights.

Professor Whitelam argues that the social and political context of Europe's re-engagement with Palestine in the nineteenth century influenced profoundly our understanding of ancient Palestine. The region was of central strategic value to the European powers, particularly with the discovery of vast oil reserves in the Gulf states. The charting of the 'new' territory, in a period of colonial expansion was by no means an act of disinterested scholarship, but was an aspect of Europe's determination to control other cultures. Moreover, Europeans investigated 'The Holy Land' virtually exclusively from the perspective of its biblical origins, in search of the taproot of their own civilisation. Their efforts coincided with European territorial ambitions, and illustrate the integral relationship between scientific investigation and its imperial supporters.

European imperialist assumptions have profoundly influenced the conventional understanding of the history of Palestine and its peoples. To a degree, biblical studies and archaeology shared European imperialism's set of assumptions. Rather than being a region with its own intrinsic value, Palestine was primarily the location of the biblical events, and as a mere backdrop to the Bible, the wider Palestinian history was silenced. Nineteenth-century European biblical scholars, sharing their society's developmentalist views of civilisation, saw it as natural that a more primitive Canaanite religion and society were inevitably replaced by a more developed (Israelite) one. Evolution progressed inexorably, and reached its pinnacle in the European nation state, a system which in their minds had reached a level of adulation bordering on worship. Each stage of the cultural development of ancient societies was superseded by the next stage, as it progressed towards its purposeful, developmentalist goal. Europe's self-consciousness regarding the inherent superiority of its civilisation and its place as the pinnacle of cultural development was confirmed by the world-wide extension of its power. Biblical scholarship shared the prevailing values in being dismissive of indigenous cultures, and viewing them as unworthy, immoral, corrupt, or primitive. The Zionist movement also was a product of such a climate.

The West's preoccupation with the Bible, and with the history of 'Ancient Israel' in particular has silenced the wider regional history of ancient Palestine. Moreover, it has resulted also in reconstructions of ancient Palestinian history which have virtually mirrored the modern struggle for Palestine. Rather than being a picture of the real past, 'Ancient Israel' was transposed into a mirror image of the present. Jerusalem was made to have no past earlier than the period of David, and any Palestinian history prior to the emergence of 'Ancient Israel' or Davidic Jerusalem was eliminated in biblical scholarship, with the result that the periods from the Neolithic to the Late Bronze Age were accorded no intrinsic value of their own. These real historical periods were reduced to the status of a 'pre-', or 'proto-history' leading up to the emergence of 'Ancient Israel' and the period of David in the Iron Age, and their populations became mere progenitors of 'biblical Israel'.

Palestine must be allowed to be more than a mere museum of Europe's antecedents, and its history deserves to be investigated in its own right, free of Eurocentric domination. For example, it has been a core assumption of biblical studies until very recently that the kingdom (or even 'empire') of David, like its later European counterparts, reached the pinnacle of political evolution in becoming a nation state. However, that there was a major state, let alone an empire, centred on Jerusalem in the tenth century BC has been undermined by the absence of archaeological evidence of the significant structures necessary to administer such a territory.

The conventional reading of the history of the region, then, has yielded a distorted picture, with the character of a scarcely known past filled in by details deriving from the present. This picture was superimposed on the real past by a particular reading of the biblical traditions, and by the influence of European, and later Israeli scholars, who read their perceptions of the modern nation state into the past, imposing the language of the modern state on the ancient political arrangements: it was purely defensive, and was a civilising influence in the region, set apart from its neighbours. The main support for this fabricated reconstruction has been completely undermined by the researches of the Israeli archaeologist, Israel Finkelstein, who has shown that the most important archaeological 'evidence' is much later than the period of David and Solomon, with the result that the 'nation-state' of David, traditionally considered to be the pinnacle of political evolution in the region, assumes more modest proportions. Such archaeological evidence radically alters our understanding of the history of Jerusalem also. Findings of that kind stimulate an exciting phase in the study of ancient Palestine, which ultimately will lead to a complete reappraisal of the historical, cultural, and political circumstances that obtained there from the thirteenth century onwards. The new history of Palestine will accord due place to the cultures and religious achievements of all the peoples of the region.

And there were many peoples, each of whom, despite the portrayal of them in the biblical narrative, constituted a culture of considerable distinction. Professor Thompson argues that the authority for the politically volatile and competitive claims of Palestinians and

Israelis about the past is biblical, rather than historical. Truth requires us to listen to the Bible's own critique of the claim to exclusive ownership of the land, in its presentation of ancient Israel as the false Israel.

Thompson argues that the concept of ethnicity in general, whether applied to Jews or Palestinians of the past or present, is a fiction created by writers. It is a political, rather than an anthropological aspect of human society, and is a product of history writing, and as such is owned by those who write it. In the case of the history of Palestine and the history of Israel the owners are European historiographers. Europeans have written this history, for Europe's own purposes, namely, to trace the progressive development of its own self-identity 'from the Stone Age to Christianity'.

To all intents and purposes, the Bible's story was made to define Palestine's history. The victims of this Bible-based, European-crafted historiographical enterprise are the outsiders to the groups defined as significant by Bible and embraced by European historiographers in search of their own origins. While it is well known that European historiography regarded the post-apostolic Christian and Islamic communities in Palestine as outsiders to its self-definition, more recently it is becoming obvious that it excludes also many of the peoples who inhabited the region from the Early Bronze Age to the end of the second century. The Bronze Age became merely an historical introduction to the Bible, the succeeding Iron Age was described almost by way of a paraphrase of the Bible, and the six centuries between Nebuchadnezzar and Jesus were treated simply as a dark age.

The modern European concept of 'nation-state', a not innocuous political arrangement considering that it has been responsible for mass slaughter in this century, has been imposed upon the Iron Age societies of Syria and Palestine, thereby distorting the real past of the Iron Age in the service of European self-identity. In fact, Bronze or Iron Age Palestine consisted of political structures of small-region, patronage-based associations, whose diverse inhabitants should not be described as 'Canaanite' during the Bronze Age, as contrasting with 'Israelite' and 'Philistine' of the Iron Age period. Such politically motivated distortions of the history of the region, which predicates an ethnic identity of its inhabitants in antiquity, reflects a systemic bad faith in the historiography of Palestine, and should be abandoned forthwith. It is becoming clearer that the Bible is early Judaism's, and early Christianity's book, rather than ancient Israel's book.

4

When one examines the region of Syria and Palestine in the Early Bronze Age period, one finds no coherent, trans-regional political structures, but rather a heartland of villages, controlled by autonomous patrons in co-operation and competition with each other. Nevertheless, the biblical origin stories focus on a distinctive people, living in its own land, with its own language, religion and history, and historians, relying on rationalised paraphrases of the biblical narratives, assert the historicity of an originating unity which first bound an historical Israel together as a people. However, the biblical assertion of an invasion of nomads from the desert, for example, is without historical support. It is important, then, to acknowledge that it is the biblical narrative which provides the much sought-after coherence and continuity of one, distinctive race.

The historical picture also excludes a setting for Israel's origins in the Late Bronze-Iron Age transition period, and in the contrast between the highlands and the lowlands. The highlands were largely empty of settlement during the Late Bronze Age, and when new settlement came we have several historical developments that are never co-ordinated. Jerusalem is not known to have been occupied at all in Iron I, with the result that there is no room in history for a United Monarchy there. It was only after the destruction of Lachish in 700 BC that Jerusalem became a regional town. The central highlands were unified around Samaria sometime in the ninth century, and became a stable patronate until 722 BC, when it came directly under Assyrian administration. Whatever sense it enjoyed of being a nation was seriously undermined by Assyrian and Babylonian, and later, Hellenistic deportation practices. The southern hills also had little coherence. The Assyrian and Babylonian deportations, and the imposition of new settlers in Jerusalem by the Persians prevented any substantial continuity or coherent ethnic development. The imperial province of Jehud was no more reflective of a people than other Persian provinces. Moreover, the term Jehud, while originally signifying a geographic unity, took on a religious self-identity centred on a relationship with Yahu/Yahweh. The *Jehudim*, then, were not residents of Judea but members of a religious association of Yahweh affiliates, transplanted to Jerusalem, who assumed the task of creating a 'new Israel' based on the *Torah* of Yahweh. This 'new Israel' rejected the past and chose the way of Yahweh, and thus became a religious, rather than an ethnic category. Moreover, the concept of *benei Yisrael* ('children of

5

Israel') as a self-identifying metaphor of early Judaism was a concept that was created in the process of the Bible's formation.

Professor Thompson reminds us that after Jerusalem was destroyed by Roman troops in 70 AD people picked up their lives, and did so again after Bar Kochba's revolt in the second century. When the vast majority of the population of Palestine and Syria became Christian during the Byzantine period, no vast numbers were driven out, and the indigenous population continued with a transformed understanding of itself and its religion. Similarly, in the seventh century, when the vast majority of the population of Palestine and Syria became Muslim, few were driven from the land. Though many churches and synagogues became mosques, the indigenous population continued with a transformed understanding of itself and its religion.

My own enquiry focuses on the moral dimension of the land traditions of the Bible. The divine promise of land is integrally linked with the mandate to exterminate the indigenous people. Manifestly these traditions pose fundamental moral questions, when viewed by the standards of international law and conventions on human rights, more especially when their literary form is considered to be history. But whatever their literary genre, or the circumstances of their composition, these biblical traditions have fuelled virtually every form of Western colonialism, most recently the Zionist conquest of Palestine. Yet, biblical scholars pay virtually no attention to the ethical dimensions of the discussion. For their part, scholars of other relevant disciplines eschew any reference to the God-question, with the result that we are left with a series of truncated discourses, each peddling its own grasp of wisdom, with none respecting the complexity of the total question.

A more comprehensive discourse requires that participants take account of dimensions of the issue that go beyond their own specialisation. Professor Quigley's insistence on the relevance of the principles and practice of international law and the conventions on human rights are apposite. He contends that the fate of the Palestine Arabs who have been displaced from Jerusalem must be an integral part of the current Israel-PLO negotiations. According to the 1993 Declaration of Principles, these negotiations are to be conducted on the basis of UN Security Council Resolution 242, which calls for a 'just settlement' of the question of the displaced Palestine Arabs. In international law, such displaced persons have a two-fold right of return, one deriving from the body of law on nationality. A country must allow its nationals to reside within its territory, and the other country has the right to demand that the person be re-admitted to his/her own country. Moreover, rights are held also by the individual, with each person having the right to reside in his/her own country. A country refusing to re-admit one of its nationals violates his/her rights. Even though the right of return is guaranteed also in various regional conventions, Israel maintains that the displaced Palestine Arabs have no right of return, on the basis that they are not nationals of Israel.

The situation is complicated with respect to those displaced from Jerusalem. Although Israel claims sovereignty over both the western and eastern sectors of the city, the international community has not recognised its claim, and in particular considers its occupation of eastern Jerusalem to be unlawful. Moreover, the UN rejects Israel's claim that 'Jerusalem, complete and united' is 'the capital of Israel', reflected in most countries' refusal to locate their embassies there. Israel argues that displaced Jerusalemites have no right of return because Jerusalem is now Israel's. However, under international law the attachment of an individual to a territory is not affected by a change in sovereignty. Under international law, residents automatically gain the nationality of a new sovereignty, unless they decide not to accept it.

Although a district court in Israel ruled that every individual was a national of Israel provided he/she resided there at the time of the declaration of the state, the government refuses to apply it to the displaced Palestine Arabs. Moreover, Israel's argument that a return of Palestine Arabs to Jerusalem or elsewhere might undermine its authority, or threaten its security has no validity under international law as reasons to deny them the right of return. Israel has also alleged as a reason to deny the right that the Palestine Arabs left voluntarily. However, Israel is responsible under international law for the exodus of Arabs from Jerusalem, since many were forced out by violence and the threat of violence in 1948 and again in 1967. The Jerusalemites who were displaced have not only a right to return, but a right to compensation. But even if it were true that they left voluntarily, such a consideration does not invalidate the right of return.

Recently, the government of Prime Minister Netanyahu, for reasons of 'demographic security', rejected the right of return to any part of the Land of Israel west of the Jordan River. But this rationale, which amounts to discrimination on ethnic grounds, also has no basis in law. The return of displaced persons is viewed by the UN as an essential component of a settlement agreement when people have been displaced, and the General Assembly in 1948 called on Israel to repatriate displaced Palestinians, and repeated it in even stronger terms since. The UN has taken a similar position in other conflicts. The Security Council insists that the displaced persons have a right to return, and that the governmental authorities are legally obligated to repatriate them. Unfortunately in the case of Palestine, the UN is leaving the matter of repatriation to negotiations between the parties. Professor Quigley cautions that any agreement about the future of Jerusalem must provide for the repatriation of the displaced Jerusalemites, on the double ground that such a provision is not only wise politically, but is required by international law.

The distinctive perspective of my own project of applied biblical exegesis is its concern for morality and acceptable human behaviour. I insist that biblical scholars ought not to evade the contemporary issues of land in Palestine, and that their discipline must set its own house in order, since the religious and academic communities which promulgate the land traditions must shoulder some of the responsibility for the use made of them. History's ongoing identification with the warring scenes of the Hebrew Bible is a burden the biblical tradition must bear. It is the narratives themselves, rather than the sophisticated exegesis of them, which have fuelled colonial adventures and perdure as an instrument of oppression. The fact that these traditions have inspired violence for millennia makes investigation of them a crucial task. There must be a way of reading these traditions which rescues the Bible from being a blunt instrument of oppression, and acquits God of the charge of being the Great Ethnic-Cleanser.

1

WESTERN SCHOLARSHIP AND THE SILENCING OF PALESTINIAN HISTORY

Keith W Whitelam

Introduction

Europe's re-engagement with the Middle East and Palestine from the eighteenth and nineteenth centuries onward brought an increasing stream of professional explorers, often connected with the military. It included wealthy individuals, religious pilgrims, and academics, professional and amateur, who were particularly interested in the exploration of Palestine as the setting of biblical events. This re-engagement and the increasing academic as well as popular interest in the region was set in the context of Western imperial expansion. It followed, of course, in the wake of Napoleon's campaigns in Egypt, and took place against the backdrop of European territorial ambitions and intrigue. The development of a growing tourist industry, made possible by the steamship, was fuelled by reports and artistic representations of what was generally referred to as the Holy Land.

Napoleon's campaigns in Egypt had been accompanied by an army of cartographers, engineers, scientists and academics in the

Commission of Arts and Sciences. They investigated, recorded, collected and classified information about Egypt that formed the basis of France's colonial rule. The product of their labours, the ambitious *Description de l'Egypte* published at the beginning of the nineteenth century, was both an important scientific record of Egyptian customs, life, culture and history, *and* an essential element in the imperial strategy. The concern to classify and order was a necessary element in the study and control of other cultures. This is not to deny the scientific value of the multitude of travellers' reports and later archaeological excavations which emerged from Palestine and elsewhere in the wake of the Napoleonic campaigns, but it helps to illustrate the essential point of this paper, that the European re-engagement with Palestine was located in a particular historic moment which helped to shape the investigation and understanding of the history of Palestine in profound ways that are only now beginning to be unravelled. If you will bear with me, I will try to spell out how European attitudes have shaped the study of the history of the region, and then briefly show how these ideas, which have dominated much of scholarship in unseen ways, are beginning to unravel.

It is well known that many of the early travellers in the Middle East who reported back to interested audiences in Europe's capitals were in the employ of the military. The great regional survey of Palestine carried out by Conder and Kitchener in 1880, their *Map of Western Palestine in 26 Sheets from Surveys conducted for the Committee of the Palestine Exploration Fund,* helps to illustrate the point about the integral relationship between scientific study and the imperial context. Their maps of the region form an essential element in the development of the historical geography of Palestine. Yet both men were in the British Army in the pay of the British government, just like Burckhardt, credited with being the first European to visit Petra, who, disguised as Arab in pay of the British African Association, began his journey in Syria with the ultimate aim of continuing through Egypt and southward in search of the source of the Niger. He supplied information on the sacred sites of Syria-Palestine, but also on its geography which was vital for invasion and military control, its mineral deposits for commercial exploitation, its political and religious divisions, effective rulers, strong tribes, and its most powerful religious groups. In a period of European colonial expansion, the exploration of the Middle East, the mapping of the region, the recording of its ancient monuments, or the description of its inhabitants and their practices were not acts of disinterested scholarship. The land bridge of Palestine between three continents was of central strategic value to the European powers as it had been throughout antiquity and has continued to be, particularly with the discovery of vast oil reserves in the Gulf states.

It may be too simplistic to say that biblical studies, and what was to become biblical archaeology, walked hand in hand with imperialism, but the larger political and social context in which these studies were carried out, their effects upon contemporary populations, and the way in which scholarly discourse about the history of ancient Palestine was shaped and continues to be shaped, should not be ignored. Scholarship, whether biblical studies, history, archaeology, or whatever, is socially embedded and both affects and is effected by the wider social and political climate in which it is carried out. The professional and amateur explorers, artists, biblical scholars, and archaeologists, virtually all from the upper and middle classes, brought with them a set of shared assumptions that not only shaped what they found and how they represented it to professional and lay audiences back in the West, but have continued to have unseen effects on the study of the history of ancient Palestine to the present day. The attitude of superiority which shaped the reporting is evident in the many well known travellers' reports. Their concern with Palestine was as the location of the biblical events rather than one springing from an interest in the region for its own sake. It was here that they hoped to find their own roots. In essence, very often Palestine and Palestinian history were emptied of any real meaning, and were, as Melman (1992) says 'dehistoricized', or, as I would put it, 'silenced': their primary significance was as a backdrop to and illustration of the Bible (see Whitelam 1996: *passim*). For Western audiences, keen to experience what they saw as the roots of their own civilisation, they wanted to know about the history of ancient Israel rather than the wider history of ancient Palestine. This concern with the development of the scholarly encounter from the nineteenth century onwards is not just an interesting exercise in the study of the history of scholarship, but is an essential exercise in trying to understand the history of the past, in this case the history of ancient Palestine, and how it might be investigated in the present and future to give a more rounded and representative picture of the many peoples who contributed to its rich tapestry. The way the past is understood invariably has very important consequences for the present.

The truth of the shared assumptions which these academics, soldiers, pilgrims, and travellers brought with them was so self-evident to them that they did not need to be discussed. Thus they became all the more important because they were not set out in scholarly works in order to be discussed or criticised. Unless we understand these assumptions and the ways in which they worked, it is not possible to offer any kind of alternative understanding of the history of the region and its peoples which can challenge those which have grown up focusing only on ancient Israel. These scholars were the products of Victorian societies permeated with an inherent belief in developmentalist views of civilisation and society so that it was natural for them to believe that Canaanite religion and society were inevitably replaced by Israelite religion and society. The commanding assumption in all this was the belief in the nature of Progress as evidenced by the triumph of the European nation state. Albert Hourani even refers to 'the worship of the nation-state' among Western historians of the period (1980: 136). This was accompanied by a strong belief in the evolutionary development of society whereby each species, race, or civilisation, rose to new heights before making way for its successor. This broad model of developmentalism, particularly influenced by early German embryology, permeated virtually all academic disciplines, from history and anthropology to geology and the sciences. So biblical studies, from its modern inception was imbued with a domain assumption that each stage of development is inexorably superseded as the whole system is driven towards its purposeful goal. Thus George Ernest Wright, one of the major American biblical scholars of this century, could write, as late as 1950, that ancient Israel was a unique entity that naturally replaced the pagan and decadent indigenous Canaanite culture that preceded it (Wright 1950: 7-11). A self-confident Victorian society saw the spread of European power as a confirmation of its self-belief in the inherent superiority of its own civilisation and its place at the pinnacle of cultural development. The rise of Victorian anthropology, drawing on the work of sixteenth and seventeenth century anthropologists, confirmed that 'primitive' cultures had been succeeded and surpassed, just as the period of reptiles had been superseded by the age of mammals. So Sir James Frazer (1896: 162), writing in *Psyche's Task,* was able to state: 'For by comparison with civilised man the savage represents an arrested or rather retarded style of development, and an examination of his customs and beliefs accordingly supplies the same sort of evidence of the evolution of the human mind that an examination of the embryo supplies of the evolution of the human body' (cited in Bowler 1989: 37). Stephen Jay Gould's fascinating study (1984) of such ideas illustrates just how pervasive they were in shaping the attitudes of politicians and intellectuals. Their belief in the objectivity of scientific measurement meant that doubts or questions about such fundamental attitudes to their own superiority and the superiority of their own political systems were never seriously entertained or questioned. Perhaps one of the most extreme examples of how this was applied to the history of Palestine can be found in the words of the Bishop of Salisbury in 1903:

> Nothing, I think, that has been discovered makes us feel any regret at the suppression of Canaanite civilisation by Israelite civilisation ... The Bible has not misrepresented at all the abomination of Canaanite culture which was superseded by the Israelite culture (cited by Said 1992: 79).

Similarly, the American archaeologist William Foxwell Albright, the greatest biblical archaeologist of this century, attempted to justify the biblical practice of *herem* whereby the whole population of a city was put to the sword. He justifies this on the basis that

> From the impartial standpoint of a philosopher of history, it often seems necessary that a people of markedly inferior type should vanish before a people of superior potentialities, since there is a point beyond which racial mixture cannot go without disaster (Albright 1957: 280-81).

These passages may be the most extreme case of dehumanisation which I have come across but their sentiments are by no means isolated in the history of biblical scholarship. Biblical scholarship to a large extent has also remained blind to the indigenous population; all too often when it is acknowledged, it is dismissed as unworthy, immoral, corrupt, or primitive, thereby denying it any rightful claim to serious consideration. But it is a view that has been replicated in less extreme forms in Western scholarship over a long period of time.

It is, therefore, important to recognise that however diligent and skilled the biblical scholars and archaeologists who brought to life the ancient past for their western audiences were, they too were influenced by the tremendous cultural, political, and intellectual forces which shaped what they looked for, what they found, and how they interpreted it. Elie Kedourie's description of Stratford Canning is illustrative: '[His] confidence and sturdy optimism astonish. He believed that there were certain truths about politics and society vouchsafed to him, truths applicable to all climates and ages, the recognition of which brought happiness to men and their disregard misery.' Informed by his view of the Bible and English Liberalism, Canning believed that progress was inevitable. Kedourie continues, 'He laid down, by and large, the terms in which the Middle Eastern problem has been discussed till the present day' (Kedourie 1978:14). The same is true of most scholars, and politicians.

Walid Khalidi in an address in London at the beginning of 1996 also drew attention to the importance of understanding culture influences on Western attitudes to Palestine (1996: 20-24). He argued that the Balfour Declaration had to be understood in relation to the intellectual conditions arising from the Reformation and the rise of Protestantism, with its heavy emphasis on the Old Testament which had a profound influence on nineteenth century understanding of the history of the region and the development of the Zionist movement. The Zionist movement, of course, grew out of the intellectual climate which I have described. It thereby inherited the set of shared assumptions—the notion of the triumph of the nation state, the inevitable progress of society, and its sense of history—which had constrained the vision of European visitors to Palestine. The outcome is that these intellectual movements from the Reformation to nineteenth century Protestantism, in Khalidi's delightful phrase, 'arrested the history of Palestine with the Old Testament' (1996: 22). The West's concern with the Bible and trying to understand the roots of its own civilisation has resulted in a narrow focus on the history of ancient Israel and less concern with trying to understand the wider regional history of ancient Palestine. More particularly, it also resulted in reconstruction of ancient Palestinian history which often mirrored the contemporary struggles for Palestine from the early twentieth century onwards. The picture they painted of ancient Israel was little more than mirror images of their own time rather than a reflection of anything that happened in the past.

Representing the History of Jerusalem and Palestine

Let me try to demonstrate with some illustrative examples how this set of shared ideas has had such a profound effect in the presentation and understanding of the history of ancient Palestine in general and of Jerusalem in particular. Notice for example the opening statement of John Gray's *History of Jerusalem:*

> The lack of political cohesion in Palestine and Syria has always been notorious, so that it is simpler to write a history of individual cities in this region than of the land and its people. As the capital of the first considerable national state in the land, where the worship of Israel was first concentrated in Solomon's Temple, Jerusalem is the focus of important interests and ideologies, which invest it with quite a peculiar significance among all the cities of its age, and redeem its history from the merely local (Gray 1969:13)

This quotation is noteworthy for a number of reasons. It is the opening lines of a detailed history of Jerusalem written by the then Professor of Hebrew and Semitic Languages at the University of Aberdeen. Gray was one of the most eminent British biblical scholars of his time, noted for his painstaking and careful philological and historical studies. Like the scientists studied by Stephen Jay Gould, Gray was undoubtedly an eminent scholar concerned with objectivity and detachment. His opening sentences were written, according to the date of the preface, in December 1967, at the time of the loss of East Jerusalem. Yet there is no mention of the momentous political events at the time of the book's completion either in the preface, or in the final chapter entitled 'A City Divided', which covers the period of the British Mandate from 1922 to its collapse. Surprisingly, although this final chapter offers an even-handed analysis of the events leading up to the division of the city on 1948, Gray manages to steer well clear of any explicit political comment on the events of his own day when the manuscript was being completed for publication. He provides, seemingly, a model of detachment and objectivity like all good British biblical scholars. But it is for these reasons that the quotation is so noteworthy because, despite his sensitivity to the conflicting claims to

15

Jerusalem, despite his attempts at objectivity, the opening sentences illustrate perfectly the set of shared assumptions which influenced the way in which politicians and academics understood historic and contemporary Palestine. They illustrate how the history of ancient Palestine was effectively silenced or arrested in Western scholarship.

The history of the region is effectively 'dehistoricized', its history is taken away, since in Gray's view it was only Jerusalem's status as the capital of David, the capital of what he called 'the first considerable national state in the land' which, again in his terms, was able to 'redeem it from the merely local'. Local Palestinian history was of little concern, its 'peculiar significance' for Gray and others was how it related to their understanding of biblical history. Here is the triumph of the European nation state, the pinnacle of political evolution, read back into the past. Notice also that it is contrasted with 'the lack of political cohesion' in Palestine and Syria prior to this time. This is a common and influential idea particularly stemming from the work of the German scholar Albrecht Alt in the 1920s and 1930s who argued that because the indigenous cultures of the Late Bronze Age were incapable of national consciousness or political cohesion, they were swept away by ancient Israel which had developed to this level. Interestingly, this is a mirror of similar claims at the beginning of Zionist immigration during the same period when it was common to claim that the indigenous population was incapable of Arab national consciousness, despite the work of George Antonius and others since. These two sentences from Gray then encapsulate brilliantly the set of shared assumptions that have helped to shape the presentation of Palestine in Western scholarship over the last century or more. It becomes clear that however objective scholars like Gray have tried to be, they cannot easily escape the influences of their own time and society.

The interplay between scholarship and the wider politics of its own day is also revealed in the influential use of language. So for example many scholars have referred to ancient Israel at the beginning of the Iron Age as in search of a 'homeland': an echo of course from the Balfour Declaration. It was even said by one scholar that Israel was the first and only people to make Palestine its 'natural homeland' (Aharoni 1982: 90). The fact that sophisticated cultures had existed in Palestine for centuries prior to this does not seem to qualify for the idea that it might also be *its inhabitants'* natural homeland.

The point I am trying to illustrate is that the same set of beliefs and ideas that informed political attitudes to the region from the time of European re-engagement onwards finds clear echoes in the biblical scholarship of the time and continues to the present. The two reinforce one another. The most extreme form of this process of 'dehistoricization' might be the 'Jerusalem 3000 celebrations' which ignore the long history of the city prior to the time of David, a history of which Gray was well aware and which he discusses. But it continues to the present and can be found in many popular and academic statements such as in F E Peters' chapter entitled 'The Holy Places' in a volume called *The City of the Great King* edited be Nitzka Rosovsky, and published just this year, where the opening sentence reads 'When Jerusalem first appears in biblical history, it is a town without a past, a newly conquered Jebusite settlement that David had made the capital of his still insecure Israelite kingdom' (Peters 1996: 37). Similarly, the book as a whole which contains a wide range of perspectives, Jewish, Christian, and Muslim, on the history and culture of Jerusalem has a chronological table at the front which begins with David's capture of Jerusalem in 1004 BCE. It is this dehistoricization of history prior to the mention of Israel or Davidic Jerusalem which has been such an important feature running as an unexamined thread throughout much biblical scholarship.

This is not to deny the tremendous scientific value of historical and archaeological investigations which have been carried out in all periods of Palestine's history, or that these studies are vital to any attempt to write a history of ancient Palestine. But in order to pursue that history as a subject in its own right, rather than as an adjunct to European history as part of the search for its own intellectual and cultural roots by a narrow focus on biblical history, it is necessary to free it from the outdated ideas that determined how the results of these studies have been interpreted. Palestine for many Victorian writers was a kind of religious curiosity shop through which they could rummage: in the words of George Adam Smith it was 'a museum of Church history … full of living as well as of ancient specimens of the subject' (1894: viii). He recounts the ancient ruins of the past through to the present and notes that after the trail of Napoleon's march and retreat we find that, '… after the long silence and crumbling of all things native, there are the living churches of to-day, and the lines of pilgrims coming up to Jerusalem from the four corners of the world' (1894: x). Palestine and its history has no intrinsic value of its own, as evidenced in the phrase 'the long silence and crumbling of all things native'; it is redeemed only by European intervention and interest. In the same way, many earlier periods of its history from Neolithic times to the Late Bronze Age are divested of meaning as they become described as the 'prehistory' to a concern with the Iron Age and the emergence of ancient Israel or the period of David. The terms 'prehistory', or even now 'proto-history' are increasingly commonly used to describe such periods.

Perhaps the most striking example I can give is the current debate among archaeologists and historians on how to understand the hundreds of rural sites which grew up in the Palestinian highlands and steppes during the period of the Late Bronze-Iron Age transition. In the past, these villages were always understood to be 'Israelite' settlements, but as it has become increasingly clear that the settlements are indigenous to the region and that there are problems of understanding them in relation to the biblical traditions, many scholars now have accepted that the label 'Israelite' is misleading, and is only one of a number of possible designations: other terms have been proposed such as 'hill country settlers', or even 'ancient Palestinians'. However, William Dever believes that if we cannot use the term 'Israelite' with absolute certainty to identify the Iron Age villagers then we ought to use the term 'proto-Israelite', on the grounds that what he calls 'the well documented' continuity of material culture in Palestine from the twelfth through the seventh/sixth centuries BCE. He argues that this continuity of culture is evident in the burial customs, house-forms, pottery, technology, etc., and constitutes what he calls a 'national Israelite material culture'. So the villagers become the progenitors of the later, what he understands as 'biblical Israel'. But again this is a means of subsuming the history of the region and earlier periods, and defining it only in relation to its understanding of the search for ancient Israel. We may not know how these villagers understood themselves, what kind of ethnic label they used to describe themselves, but archaeologists and historians are convinced that the villages represent the development of indigenous culture. In the absence of a precise label, given that scholars refer to the area as Palestine, then they should be understood as part of the complex transformation and realignment of ancient Palestinian society which took place during the period of the late Bronze-Iron Age transition throughout the region. There was not a radical break with what had gone before: it was not part of some evolutionary scheme with one culture replacing another. Terms such as 'prehistory' and 'proto-history' suggest that it is somehow removed from history, is 'dehistoricized' and has no intrinsic value of its own. Yet this is not an isolated example of the use of such terminology: thus, A Mazar, in referring to the same settlements, concedes that,

> The emergence of Israel constituted complex processes, which involved other ethnic groups as well. The settlers in the region, whatever their origin, might not have identified themselves as part of an Israelite nation in this early stage; but they are certainly part of the population groups that provided the nucleus for the rise of the Israelite state, and thus can be defined as Israelites, in the broadest meaning of the term (A Mazar 1994: 91).

Notice how again the wider history of the region is 'dehistoricized' and that it is the nation state which becomes the defining feature of any such history, and that all preceding periods become part of its pre-, or proto-history.

My final illustration, then, is concerned with this central assumption which has come down from Victorian scholarship to the present, that the kingdom of David represents a nation state which, like its later European counterparts, reached the pinnacle of political evolution. This is an idea that has dominated all studies of the region until very recently. Histories of the period invariably describe the state founded by David after the capture of Jerusalem as one of the major powers of the ancient world. Some even go so far as to talk about an 'empire' extending from the Gulf of Aqabah to the Mediterranean and from the borders of Egypt to the Lebanon range in the north. It is an understanding of the history of the region which has been a reference point in the opening lines of Gray's history of Jerusalem, as we have seen, or in the sentiments behind the Jerusalem 3000 celebrations.

However, this idea of a major state, let alone an empire, centred on Jerusalem in the tenth century BCE has been increasingly questioned in recent years. It has been undermined by the failure of the archaeological record to reveal evidence of significant structures in the region at the time which would have been required to administer and control such a territorial expansion. A few individuals, such as Thompson, Lemche, Davies and others (Garbini 1988; Jamieson-Drake 1991; Niemann 1993), have long held that the picture that has been presented in our histories does not stand on solid ground, and that the interpretation of archaeological results has been influenced by presuppositions drawn from a particular reading of the biblical traditions. But it is also an idea that has been influenced by modern history as European, and later Israeli scholars, have read a picture of their own present back into the past. The same language which is used of the modern state is applied also to this ancient state: it is said to be only defensive, a civilising influence in the region, or a nation set apart from its neighbours. The past and the present are seen as being almost identical. A recent thorough review of the main planks in the argument by the archaeologist Israel Finkelstein has completely undermined the case (1996). He has proposed a new dating, based on a review of Philistine pottery, which means that many of the most important structures, such as the gate complexes at Megiddo, Hazor, and Gezer, cannot be dated to the time of David and Solomon and must be much later.

This means that what has conventionally been represented as the pinnacle of political evolution in the region, the nation-state of David, virtually disappears. Thus this opens up the discussion again in terms of examining this period from the perspective of a wider regional history, the processes at work, etc., reflecting an appreciation of the achievements and challenges of ancient Palestinian society in response to the complex factors which it faced, and how it responded to them.

It changes our whole perspective in looking at the history of Jerusalem, or the history of the region in general. We might ask why the situation has changed so significantly that an increasing number of scholars can challenge the understanding of the history of ancient Palestine in such a radical way? In the case of the argument about the nature of Jerusalem in the tenth century, as the centre of a major state, it is not as if the basic data have changed significantly in recent years. There have not been major archaeological finds which have suddenly revolutionised the history of the region overturning long-held views. What has changed, and is changing, is that the set of assumptions which were brought by the first European visitors no longer have the explanatory power for many scholars which they once had. As these shared assumptions start to be overturned, however gradually, it has become possible to offer a completely different perspective on important periods in the history of ancient Palestine.

This paper may appear to be mainly negative in trying to expose and unravel the complex of ideas which have underpinned European scholarship. But it is important to diagnose the problems accurately, understand their far-reaching implications, before one attempts to offer convincing alternative constructions of the past. What we are beginning to see is the opening of a very important and exciting period in the study of the history of ancient Palestine. My examples from the Late Bronze and Iron Ages illustrate that what is needed, and what is now beginning to emerge from different scholars, is a complete reappraisal of the historical, cultural, and political processes that took place in Palestine from the thirteenth century onwards. It is an understanding of history which, I hope, will give proper appreciation to the cultures and religious achievements of all its peoples.

2

HIDDEN HISTORIES AND THE PROBLEM OF ETHNICITY IN PALESTINE[1]

Thomas L Thompson

E thnicity is a political, not an anthropological aspect of human society. This is easily illustrated by a point which this audience will appreciate, which my colleague in Copenhagen Niels Peter Lemche once made, about one of the legendary founders of Israel: Omri the son of a nobody, who, in the biblical tradition, first established the northern kingdom's ancient capital by building the city of Samaria. Assyrian texts refer to ancient historical Israel as Bit Humri. Omri also shows up as the eponymous representative of Israel's armies in the famous Mesha inscription in which King Mesha complains of Israelite

---

[1] Some view these largely historical questions of antiquity in terms of the volatile and violence-prone dispute between Palestinians and Israelis, involving their competitive historical claims to a homeland, often referred to with intentions of exclusivity as Palestine or Eretz Israel. I wish to address very explicitly this contentious historical issue. The only justification I offer for this paper is my obligations to the field as an historian and biblical scholar. The authority for such politically volatile claims about the past is not historical but biblical, and if we are truthful about that, we must also listen to the Bible's critique of this claim in its presentation of ancient Israel as the false Israel. The voice of this critique is neither Christian nor Islamic but that of early Judaism.

raids on his territory. It is an irony that the name Omri and its Assyrian form, Humri are obvious West and East Semitic renderings of the well known Arabic name, *Omar.* To that great fictive Omar, the eponymous founder and patron of the house of Omar, the small Iron Age highland patronate called Israel which ruled from the town of Samaria, I would like to dedicate this paper.[2] My thesis, that ethnicity is a political, not an anthropological aspect of human society, is no less true of Jews and Palestinians—today as in the past—than of any people. The concept of ethnicity is a fiction, created by writers. It is a product of literature: a product of history writing. As such it is owned by those who do the writing.

This capacity and vulnerability of tradition for creative reinterpretation is not bound by the tradition's content nor by its ties to the past. It is determined by the bearers of tradition; namely by those who claim the tradition as their own. Far too little attention has been paid to this question of the self-identifying bearers of tradition which lies so close to the heart of history writing.

Eurocentric History

The history of Palestine and the history of Israel is European history. Europeans have written it and they have written it for Europe's own purposes. The pre-emptive claims on the history of Palestine and on the history of Israel supports European intellectual and spiritual claims of continuity with the Bible and its past. Europe's self-identity as Christian has an origin story in the Bible that reaches back to creation, or, as Albright put it, from the Stone Age to Christianity. But European self-understanding is not restricted to the biblical myths of origin, neither to that of the old Israel of the garden story of the Book of Genesis, nor to the new Israel of the prologue of John's Gospel. It has also

---

[2] That Omar, like David, the eponymous founder of Byt Dwd, the dynastic patronate of Iron Age Jerusalem, is a fictive eponymic founder of Bit Humri is argued in Thompson 1995; for some of the problems of seeing either the biblical or the Mesha view of Omri/Humri as historical see Sjeggestad 1993: 103-106. Further on this see my forthcoming 'Gleanings from Niels Peter Lemche's 1996 Kohlhammer textbook, *Die Vorgeschichte Israels,* where the literary genre of the Mesha inscription is discussed.

been profoundly influenced by the myth of history: that myth which offers us a world of the past as it actually happened. It is in this context, I believe, that the European claims on Palestine's past are most tenacious.

Comparable to Europe's claims on the Bible have been its claims of cultural and intellectual heritage of classical Greece and Hellenism, as Europe again and again places its spiritual roots in the Roman imperium. The barbarism of the early Middle Ages, before Averroes and Avicenna lent themselves to Europe's re-education, is a dark period of our history which only Scandinavians can feed on with nostalgia. The pre-emptive assertion of classical roots creates an identity that touches every aspect of European cultural reflection. Europe and the West's historical claims to the intellectual and spiritual property of ancient Syria and Palestine are rooted in fourth century Christianity's rediscovery of its religious roots in Palestine, reflected, for example, in the nostalgic researches into early biblical antiquities from St Helena to Jerome, which gave us both Jerusalem's Via Dolorosa and the first Western Bible. The contemporary depth of such imperial aspirations with which Europe still educates its young finds its origins in the reforming traditions of the Renaissance and the Enlightenment: the first crowned by the Protestant revolt which asserted the Bible's place in the moral and spiritual life of everyman, as the latter was marked by the paradigm of history at the centre of the European understanding of reality. The past speaks directly to us through the living of its old world-creating god, and it is Europe that controls that past world, and its god, with a firm hand on history's creative force.

For example, Napoleon's troops marked the beginning of modern scholarship's interest in the Middle East, and this imperialistic nostalgia of historical and archaeological scholarship has led to a reassertion of Europe's rights over Palestine's past, both as part of our own vision of our patrimony in a civilisation which is seen as having developed progressively over now 5000 years, as well as part of a religious struggle within the West among Christians for intellectual dominance in education. In both these efforts, the peculiar westernised concept of ethnicity which has hidden Palestine's past has functioned to support a chain of historic succession from the ancient Near East epitomised in the Hebrew Bible, to Alexander's Hellenistic unities, to the New Testament and early Christianity. The primary heuristic function of such chains as this central linkage in the West's self-understanding is, of course, stability. But nostalgia—that historiographic description of the past in its function of informing us about ourselves—also creates both amnesia and myopia, because of the need to reduce the past's otherness.

Accepting the West as the lords of history comes at a price; namely, the alienation so well described in Edward Said's *Orientalism:* the price of your identity, whoever you, who call yourselves Palestinian, may be. This self-reflective perspective which characterises Western historicism is reflected in the Hegelian progressive evolutionary perspectives so central to European scholarship's lack of self-criticism. This ideology Said has criticised and Whitelam has described as conducive to a blindness to Palestine's hidden histories.

The history of international scholarship's neglect of post-apostolic Christian and Islamic periods in Palestine is well recognised. What have not been so recognised prior to Keith Whitelam's book are the many considerable and unnecessary gaps in our history from the Early Bronze Age to the end of the second century, and it is these hidden histories I would like to address. As archaeological and historical scholarship transformed the Bible's story into Palestine's history—from the Bronze Age's *Palestine Before the Hebrews* (Anati 1968), to Jerusalem's destruction by the Babylonian army—it transformed both the Bronze Age and the Iron Age in the process. The Iron Age became a rationalised paraphrase of the Bible: a secular Bible if you will, and the Bronze Age served as an historical introduction to the Bible: important not in itself but for what followed. But these were the lucky periods. For many, the history of Palestine ended in the sixth century BCE. The six centuries between Nebuchadnezzar and Jesus belong to hidden history: and hidden within that period is also Judaism's beginnings and the Bible's origins. This was tolerable within the old paradigm, as this period was understood as a dark age. It was a period of transition: a period of preparation leading up to Christianity. This is not a Jewish history, however much Zionist politically-motivated education might exploit it. Nothing of interest lies between the 'Old' and 'New' Testaments. The Roman period is saved for Jesus' sake, but after the Jewish rebellions of 70 and 135, Western enthusiasm follows the cross westwards, marking the path of its own self-understanding.

Essential to the Western Christian understanding is the theological competitive and sectarian claim of being the New Jerusalem and the New Israel: the legitimate heir of biblical faith. The coherence rendered historical communities by the unifying designations of ethnicity is central to the development of this Christian understanding of history, in which the many have become one in Jesus Christ. Correspondingly, the distortive thrust of this historiographical view centres in the sectarian theology of the biblical view of nations. I will return to this theme.

Ethnicity as Fiction

In the twentieth century the concept of *ethnos* or 'nation', even more than race or religion, has been a very dangerous fiction, responsible for more deaths in this one century than there ever were lives in antiquity. Although I consider it necessary to bring to mind the millions slaughtered in the name of nationalism, and especially the efforts of German fascism to destroy Europe's Jews and gypsies, I do not wish to focus on the specific evils of this concept of nationalism and ethnicity when linked to military power, whether totalitarian or democratic, but rather upon its meaning and appropriateness for speaking about peoples of antiquity. Fascism's Nordic racism was much more closely linked to pan-European imperialist perspectives which are more comparable to Edward Said's 'Orientalism', than it is to that process of self-identity among peoples that we refer to with the concepts of 'nation' and 'ethnos', which may adhere to many different forms and aspects of social organisations. A concept of 'nation-state' that owed much to Wilsonian perceptions of political and social realities of the post-imperial world of the early twentieth century has been used to describe the Iron Age societies of Syria and Palestine ever since Albrecht Alt first established the parameters of modern critical historical research for this region in the decade following 1925 (see Alt 1925; 1930). This presupposition about Iron Age societies—namely that there were then both nations and states in Palestine—has dominated the historical perceptions of our field ever since Giorgio Buccellati published his comprehensive study, *Cities and Nations of Ancient Syria* (1967).

Such anachronistic language is not only based on a perception of ethnicity which is defined primarily as an association of politics and language. It is yet more distorting. In discussions about ancient Palestine, the anachronistic assumptions regarding nations and states reflect not the *ethnē* of the ancient world but rather that known in the great complex states which dominate Europe from France to Russia. This distortion hinders understanding of the past political forms which in fact existed during the Iron Age, just as the distortion itself is strengthened by such associations with European self-identity. This European perspective understands ethnicity as an aspect of large, complex societies which in fact have been formed by the amalgamation of many peoples. It is this concept which unfortunately encourages historians to view the great ancient political entities of Egyptian, Assyrian, Persian and Greek as 'ethnicities'. Such perceptions are so inappropriate to the ancient world that we are brought to the brink of absurdity when one attempts to write a history of Bronze or Iron Age Palestine, where political structures were ever small-region patronage-based associations (see Lemche 1985; 1991). Comprehensive terms reflect not Palestine's past but the present ideology of those who use them; such as 'Canaanite' (the Israeli archaeological term for the inhabitants of the region during the Bronze Age, in contrast to 'Israelite' and 'Philistine' as terms for the inhabitants of Palestine during the Iron Age), 'Palestinians' (Whitelam's term), and especially the ideologically pernicious 'Canaanite Arabs'. However understandable the frustration from the now considerable politically motivated manipulation of the history of this region, the existence of such distortions of the tradition reflects a systemic bad faith that is present in the historiography of our field.

The somewhat pretentious use of the term 'state' also brings disproportion to our historical imaginations. The political structures of Bronze Age Palestine are commonly characterised as 'city-states', a term which not only evokes images of Florence, Naples and Venice, but demands impossible parallels in antiquity with the ancient world's great autonomous cities: Babylon, Assur, Nineveh, Thebes, Susa, Antioch, Alexandria, Athens and Rome. Even the smaller autonomous cities of greater Syria, such as Ebla, Damascus, Byblos, Ugarit and Tyre so dwarf the small towns and villages of Bronze Age Palestine which functioned as 'capitals' of the region's patronates of Ammon and Moab, Israel and Judah, that concepts and terms such as state and city seem particularly misleading in reference to Palestine.[3] The concept of nation

---

[3] Sites such as Hazor and Dan seem hardly Palestinian, but might better be understood as towns of Syria's southern fringe. These ancient towns and the as yet unexcavated town of Gazza on the southern coast can hardly be reconciled with descriptions which subordinate them within a politically unified southern Levant.

presupposes a unity for the South Levantine region which has eluded historians ever since Alt first attempted to integrate the biblical story and archaeology.

The fragmentation of Palestine's topography is such that it can be stated unequivocally that Palestine has never been under the autonomous control of a single indigenous power in the whole of the pre-modern world. The comprehensive term 'Palestinian' as an ethnic denominator is wholly anachronistic. South Levantine states have ever had the character of secondary state structures under the domination, or functioning in the military shadow of one or other imperial power: Egypt, Assyria, Babylon, Persia, Macedonia, Rome, Byzantium, Damascus, Baghdad, Istanbul, London and Washington. During none of these periods was political and social integration ever attempted in Palestine. Interactive economies of distinct groups within the several distinct regions was ever the mark of imperial control there.

That this chain of external domination is nearly unbroken should not remain unnoticed as we discuss such concepts as *ethnos*—even the Hasmoneans in the Maccabaean interlude demonstrate the growing reach of Roman power. Such concepts of self-identity and self-understanding demand much from the fictive language of autonomy. In ancient antiquity's political world, language and its metaphors—and the political associations supporting such perceptions—were ever primarily tools of empire. It was not the centralised and absolute monarchs of Europe which ruled the ancient world, but the vicar of the divine, the kings of kings. The metaphor of 'king' in the ancient world, signifying 'autonomy', is important to understand, as it is no accident that the biblical fictive world finds so countless the kings among Palestine's scrub farmers. If the seat of government mirrors the divine king of kings, then one has to people the world—as in Grimm's and Sheharazad's tales—with as many kings and princes as possible.[4]

The concept of *ethnos* as it is commonly used by historians today distorts the past for us more than it informs; and for this reason it is time that we rid ourselves of this distortion. However, words such as *ethnē* and *goyim,* clearly reflect an ancient perspective, if not an ancient historical reality. The term itself is ancient in both its Greek and Hebrew forms. Herodotus, the early Greek collector of many of the early

---

[4] This is already reflected, for example, in the early Middle Bronze's execration texts. See the comprehensive discussion in Thompson 1974: 91-117.

traditions and stories of Asia, for example, uses this term and even defines it for us: an *ethnos* describes a single people: a specific folk, related to each other in interrelated families, with its own language and religion, its own land and history. Yet it is specifically in terms of such an understanding as offered by Herodotus that our modern perceptions can be seen as different from that of the ancients. For Herodotus, definition is essential, prescriptive and idealistic. The descriptive quality of modern definitions based on usage is entirely absent. Ancient ethnicity related to assertion and self-understanding in terms of metaphor. Ethnicity was not a descriptive aspect, describing a society, as if it were a historical 'fact' that existed objectively and impartially in some 'real' world that historians discover; but rather Herodotus' *ethnē* belong to the world of language and to the world of literature. The socially relevant genre of ethnography, of which Herodotus' writings offer us one of the earliest and greatest examples, like other narrative genres such as myth and legend, did not offer descriptions of the observable peoples which existed in Persia. Rather, Herodotus described the Persian world—the world of his travels—in terms of specific constructs within a philosophical discourse about the past.

Ethnicity and the Bible

The five elements of the early Greek ethnographers' functional definition of *ethnos*—and remember this is neither a descriptive nor empirical, but an essential description—are: 1) a united people; 2) with a common language; 3) with a defining religion; 4) in possession of a land; and, 5) with a common past and future goal. As these five elements form the essential developmental themes which are explicated in biblical narrative, one might be excused for understanding the narrative as substantially ethnographic rather than historiographic in its goal. That is to say, the biblical narrative is defining contemporary people as a very specific and coherent reality; indeed, it is creating a reality; that is, that of the 'New Israel', in a manner comparable to that of Herodotus and other early ethnographers. In this way we can speak of the Bible as an origin story: a narrative whose intention was to create an understanding of the bearers of the tradition as an *ethnos* (see Thompson 1987; 1992: 415-23).

There are, however, two important, transforming qualifications that need to be considered in dealing with this perception of the Bible as origin story. One relates to our own historical understanding of the past which forms and provides us with both contexts and potential referents of such an ethnic assertion.[5] This qualification draws us into a discussion of the fictive and intellectually creative character of biblical literature. It is also necessary to consider the theologically and philosophically critical context in which these origin narratives find themselves. I refer specifically here to the Bible's own analysis of ancient Israel as the lost Israel, both substantially and intentionally questioning the appropriateness of the very ethnicity which the Bible creates for its heuristic purposes. For the Bible is not ancient Israel's book. Rather it is early Judaism's and early Christianity's book.

I would like to consider in turn these two qualifications, based on my literary understanding of biblical Israel: first dealing with its relationship to the historical past of the southern Levant (that is, to the past as known to historians), and then, more philosophically, with regard to the Bible's own internal critique. While the biblical origin stories centre themselves in the coherence of an *ethnos*, comparable to that defined by Herodotus as a people, living in its own land, with its own language, religion and history, historians have concentrated on asserting the historicity of an originating unity which they believe must have first bound an historical Israel together as a people, using for the most part a rationalised paraphrase of one or other of the Bible narratives of Genesis-II Kings regarding each of these five unifying elements.

This issue of ethnicity runs through the very heart of the current academic debates on the early history of the southern Levant and biblical origins. The purpose of my 1992 monograph on *The Early*

---

[5] That any discussion of biblical traditions which touches upon the issue of historicity, the distinction between the text's perception and ancient history, is in danger today of polemical response is an unfortunate aspect of contemporary biblical studies: see, for example, Rainey 1995, Halpern 1995, Provan 1995 and Dever 1995; 1996. That such polemics frequently do not stop short at charges of intentional and politically motivated bias, including accusations of nihilism and the hatred of religion, of anti-Judaism and anti-Semitism, are barriers to the free exchange of ideas. Efforts since the late 1980s to develop a history of the south Levant, which was independent of the perspective of biblical historiography, and specifically a regionally oriented history, projected already in Coote and Whitelam 1987, and in Thompson, Gonçalves and Cangh 1988, have faced a response that is specifically politically, not scholarly motivated.

History of the Israelite People was to trace the origins of the coherence and unity, the self-understanding and identity that permeates biblical texts and to allow the voice of these texts to be understood as that of a people.[6] The ethnic character of the discussion of Israel's origins, and indeed the entire question of Israel's earliest history, has marked the academic discussion since Wellhausen and Eduard Meyer. This, quite simply, has been because of the basic, first requirement of identifying what the historical Israel in fact was. We had first to know what we were looking for before we could find it. This is not as simple as it sounds; for our best and most obvious source is a Hellenistic collection of texts which present a theological discussion about an ancient, lost Israel which no longer existed. These texts speak from the perspective of a people who claim a new departure from that past.

As late as 1967 the European academic world traced the original homeland of each of the Semitic peoples known in the ancient world to a series of successive migrations of nomads out from the Arabian desert (see Moscati 1967). This impossibly romantic picture hardly survives more recent scholarship, which rather understands the Semitic languages to have developed from Afro-Asiatic, and the specific evolution of the Semitic world to have originated in the migrations of the Neolithic period from as early as 6000 BCE and ending sometime before 4000 BCE. This migration of farmer-shepherds from the Green Sahara into Palestine and Syria, as the Sahara's sands spread and finally closed Egypt off from the Berber lands of the West at the end of the fifth millennium, led to a gradual integration of the immigrants from Africa with the Neolithic population in Palestine.

Again, it was not from Arabia's nomadic shepherds, but rather from Syria and Palestine's more complex Mediterranean economy that the Semitic languages spread throughout the Fertile Crescent, and developed over the centuries their unique civilisations: Akkad, Babylon and Assur in the East, Arabia to the south and finally the Aramaeans in the north and all along the desert's western fringe. With the return to a good agricultural climate during the fourth millennium, and especially with the onset of the subpluvial of the Early Bronze Age, the Mediterranean economy in Palestine and Syria was developed throughout all of Palestine-Syria's many sub-regions. This was an

---

[6] See also my 'Defining History and Ethnicity in the South Levant' in Grabbe 1997, and especially my forthcoming book, *The Bible and the Past* (London: Cape, 1998).

economy that was marked by local and regional trade and barter between the steppe-dwelling pastoralists, the highland horticulturalists who concentrated on olives and grapes, and the wheat and barley farmers of the flatlands. The economy also gave each small region its local definition and autonomy. Politically, each small local patron provided the town and its few outlying villages with markets and the protection of the fortifications which we find defending every major settlement in the land.

Such patronage is a characteristic of Palestine's political structures that was to last throughout the Bronze and Iron Ages. When one considers the Early Bronze Age for Syria and Palestine, one finds no coherent, trans-regional political structures. Rather we are clearly dealing with a heartland of villages, controlled by autonomous patrons in co-operation and in competition with each other. From a chronological perspective, one also finds a remarkable stability of population, marked by continuous regional settlement until the close of the Early Bronze Age late in the third millennium BCE, when droughts once again intensified, disrupting the entire southern region's (that is, Palestine's) economy.

Biblical and archaeological scholarship into the mid-seventies had understood this Early Bronze-Middle Bronze intermediate period in terms of the old migration theory of Semitic nomads from Arabia. Albright and Noth, linking this theory to cuneiform and Egyptian texts about *Amurru* or *Amw*, developed a history of Amorite migratory invasion which overwhelmed the whole of the ancient Near East, destroyed the Early Bronze cultures of Mesopotamia and Palestine, created Egypt's First Intermediate, and, after several centuries, led to the development of the Old Babylonian dominance of Mesopotamia and the Middle Bronze in Syria and Palestine. Albright went further and linked this 'Amorite Movement' with the tales of the biblical patriarchs, thus linking the patriarchs ethnically with this migration. It was in fact an entirely redundant double theory of quasi-nomadic origins which depended on the biblical narrative for its historical coherence: Jacob went down to Egypt, there to become Israel and return to Palestine with Joshua and a new immigration or invasion of Israelites during the Late Bronze-Iron Age transition period. The essential redundancy of Albright's theories—and not sociological perceptiveness—is what in fact lay behind Mendenhall's 1962 assertion that the Israelites were indigenous Canaanites who were moved by an immigrating Moses group to rebellion against the Canaanite city-states.[7]

Albright did not really establish an historical synthesis and reconstruction on the basis of argument, but rather asserted a harmony of linkages between the biblical narratives and historical data. The biblical narrative provided the necessary coherence and continuity. The incoherence of Albright's synthesis—and especially the need of ethnic coherence within the historical argument—encouraged Alt, and especially Noth, to view the stories of the origins of the Israelite people in terms of patriarchal origins as in Genesis, of conquest as in the Book of Joshua and of settlement as in the Book of Judges as three variants of a folk history about Israelite origins. Alt's and Noth's peaceful settlement hypothesis was driven by the need to assert ethnic unity: and this was provided in the story of Joshua 24's pan-Israelite tribal covenant: a story which seemed to be confirmed by assumptions concerning nomadic origins.

The collapse of these reconstructions has been both precipitous and definitive. With the establishment of Afro-Asiatic at the origins of proto-Semitic, both Arabia's role and the historical reality of successive migrations of Amorites and Aramaeans disappear entirely. The intermediate periods at the end of the Early Bronze Age and again at the end of the Late Bronze Age are far better explained today as internal changes in the economy and in forms of sedentarisation: as efforts to adapt to changes in climate, environment and in trade relationships on which the Mediterranean economy was dependent (see Coote and Whitelam 1987, and Thompson 1992: 316-33). The population itself was stable and resilient, using forms of both nomadism and sedentarism to purposes of considerable regional and temporal divergence; in times of ecological stress, shifting the population over an ever larger region (see Thompson 1992a).

The resilience and constancy of Palestine's population over centuries brings us directly back to the issue of ethnicity. Apart from recurrent additions to the population, such as from Arabia, Anatolia, and—during the Great Mycenaean drought—from coastal Anatolia and the Aegean, the population of the region is stable until the Assyrian period. Biblical archaeology's assertion of an invasion of nomads from

---

[7] Serious interest in sociological questions came rather by way of Gottwald's *The Tribes of Yahweh* (1979), who, however, was satisfied with minor revisions of Mendenhall's Albrightean construction.

the desert—whether of Amorites or of Aramaeans, whether of patriarchs or Joshua's army—finds no historical support whatever.

The historical picture, in fact, also excludes a setting for Israel's origins in the Late Bronze-Iron Age transition period, and in the contrast between the highlands and the lowlands (see Thompson 1992: 334-39). Apart from the ancient enclave in the interconnected highland valleys of Shechem and the settlement of Jerusalem at the head of the Ayyalon valley, the highlands were largely empty of settlement during the Late Bronze Age (see Thompson 1979). When new settlement comes into the highlands, the settlement history of the Bethlehem to Hebron hills, for instance, comes historically separate from, and chronologically later by two centuries than the new settlements of the highlands from Ramallah to Nablus. The Upper Galilee highlands are related to Phoenicia, the eastern Galilee centred around the towns of Tel Dan and Hazor, and the Lower Galilee's settlements are drawn from the Jezreel. We have not one historical development here but many: and they are never co-ordinated.

The settlement of the southern hills begins first late in the eleventh century and is closely oriented to the development of forts in the northern Negev and Judaea. Jerusalem is not known to be occupied at all in Iron I. There is no room in history for either a David or for a United Monarchy in Jerusalem. Lachish is the dominant town of the southern hills. Only after the destruction of Lachish in 700 BCE, is Jerusalem assigned the southern highlands by the Assyrians, and for the first time it become a regional town.

The central highlands, on the other hand, are newly settled already towards the end of the thirteenth century. The area is unified around Samaria sometime in the ninth century. This patronate has a stable history until 722 when, after Samaria's destruction, it comes directly under Assyrian administration. This highland patronate was called Israel and Bit Humri and was in long-standing competition with Tyre and Damascus for control of the Jezreel, and with Ammon for control of the Gilead.

If this Israel had developed any clear sense of being a nation, it was seriously undermined by Assyrian and eventually Babylonian deportation practices which transferred tens of thousands to and from the region. Such population discontinuity continued into the Hellenistic period with Alexander's settlement of Macedonians in Samaria. The self-understanding implicit in the terms *benei Yisrael* and *Shomronim* used by the later Samaritans has its roots here in a form of a reassertive ethnicity; that is, in an ideology of ethnicity that is substantially strengthened by the much later Samaritan's biblical tradition.

The southern hills, however, have very little continuity or coherence. Originally developing from frontier settlements and from the forced sedentarisation of pastoralists, the very small villages of Judah were subject to the domination of larger towns on the highland fringe: first Lachish in the Shephelah, and then Jerusalem in the Ayyalon. The Assyrian and Babylonian deportations at the end of the eighth and at the beginning of the sixth centuries were disastrous not only for Jerusalem but even more for the Judaean hills. The imposition of new settlers in Jerusalem by the Persians—returnees for ideology's sake, but all the same, foreigners and usurpers—during the fifth century prevent any substantial continuity or coherent ethnic development.

As with the Assyrians' name for the southern highlands of Judaia, the Persians' imperial province of Jehud was no more reflective of a people than other Persian provinces. Jehud itself seems to have been originally a geographic term. However, already in the Elephantine texts the name *Yehudim* is not used in its geographical sense but in the context of a religious affiliation.[8] *Yehudim* is understood already from this very early period, folk-etiologically, in terms of a self-identity centred in a religious relationship with Yahu/Yahweh. They are not residents of Judea but members of a religious association of those who centre their lives on Yahweh. So we can find people who call themselves 'Jews' in Persian period Elephantine, and find themselves 'related' to the communities associated with the temples of Samaria as also with that of Jerusalem. Certainly this is the implied self-understanding—this religious ethnicity—of the authorial voice of so many biblical texts which look back upon ancient Israel as lost and upon themselves as transplanted to Jerusalem to create a 'new Israel' centred in the Torah given to them by Yahweh, the long forgotten god of Israel past.

This 'new Israel'—like Israel's troops in Joshua 24—rejects the

---

[8] This was in a manner analogous to the Samaritan's self-identify as *Shomronim,* as is tentatively suggested by Ingrid Hjelm in her forthcoming study, *Samaritans.* That is, the *Shomronim* are not residents of Samaria or its geographical region but are to be understood as a religious affiliation. They are the 'watchers' of the *Torah,* which also may be reflected in the pseudonymous authors of Jubilees, as mythically portrayed in First Enoch, and perhaps alluded to in Psalm 1's introduction to the psalter as a function of *Torah* study.

past and chooses a new way, the way of Yahweh. This is certainly the perspective of the stories of John Hyrcanus who is seen re-establishing a new Israel throughout newly conquered lands—and here the concept of the 'land of Israel' in the books of Maccabees is a precursor of the understanding of Dar as-Salam—not through ethnic selection but through conversion. Similar is also the understanding of 'true Israel' given by the founding figure of the Dead Sea Scrolls Damascus Covenant, the 'teacher of righteousness'. It is in its essence a sectarian perspective: the true Israel is understood as those who hold to the way of truth. It is in just such a context, I think, that Josephus presents the Pharisees as Jews for the 'new Israel', in contrast to the Hasmonean anchored Sadducees who adhere to the old Israel and to the temple. However, the *sadiqim*—hardly ever to be harmonised with Josephus' group—stand solidly behind just such a sectarian defined path of righteousness as that of the 'new Israel', which is a profoundly religious, and not an ethnic definition. It is moreover, a perception and self-understanding which must force the historian not merely to speak of this region's 'many Judaisms', but rather to speak of neither Judaism nor Israel as a people at all, except in this very defining sense as a people of god. Jews, Idumaeans, Galileans and Samaritans, as well as Essenes and Pharisees: the writers of the gospels as well as the early Rabbis of the Talmud—all understood themselves with the defining term *benei Yisrael.* The gospels—with all of their seemingly anti-Semitic abuse of the term 'Jew'—are works which are centred in this sectarian and biblical view of the 'new Israel', perceiving of Judaism from a religious perspective as with the rabbis. From the perspective of antiquity, the significance of Judaism and its *Torah* lies not in the physical world of ethnicity any more than in that of the tradition's historicity, but, rather, in the understanding that the texts and their study bring.

Such understandings of the language of our traditions require that we look differently at the history we write. I have in the past argued that the concept of *benei Yisrael* as a self-identifying metaphor of early Judaism was a concept that was created in the process of the Bible's formation. Even such a unifying paraphrase is highly anachronistic in its definition of the biblical writings of the Hellenistic period as Jewish, understood ethnically as a (that is, a single) people. We need to take Whitelam's critique of the hidden histories seriously; for the religious movements which such ideology creates are many and various. They are also hardly harmonious, however structurally similar they may have been.

Rather than substituting the history of the southern Levant during the Hellenistic period with a paraphrase of First or Second Maccabees, we need to think more about Phoenicia and the Decapolis, about the towns of the lowlands and of the coast. We must especially think of Beth Shan and the towns of the Jezreel, and we must not forget the Galilee. We might also think of religious ideas and the writings of texts during the Greco-Roman period more as an intellectual and philosophical movement of Hellenism itself, rather than as a reactionary religious movement of Palestine's least Hellenised 'Jews'. Were the temples of Jerusalem, Samaria, Elephantine, Leontopolis and Beersheva expressions of religious coherence, or were they reflective of the political and religious aspirations of one or other of many factions, which might just as well be contrasted to Pharisees and Essenes as to each other? If Judaism were a religion that had its central originative core in the temple cult of Jerusalem, it could not be Samaritan; and not only not Samaritan, it could not even be Judaean understood geographically and ethnically. Similarly, if kingship continued to be an epitomising factor of patronage, what was the significant factor of Idumaean power in Judaea, especially regarding their sponsor's relationship to Jerusalem's temple? Certainly many early texts—such as the sectarian literature in the Dead Sea Scrolls—do not see the temple as the core of their religion, albeit they do recognise its political and cultic value. Similarly, Elephantine texts indicate that the Jerusalem and Samaritan temples are both important non-monopolistic centres of their understanding of 'Judaism'. And how do the groups of Galileans fit in? If Idumeans and Galileans can be understood as *Yehudim,* what of the people of the Transjordan from Philadelphia to Damascus?

Could all who adhered to such a religion understand themselves as 'Jews', or, like the Samaritans, as *benei Yisrael.* The LXX is associated with the 'Jews' of Alexandria. Were they originally transported from Alexander's Samaria, or were they 'Jews' because of their biblical faith? And where did the Jews of the Jerusalem Talmud come from: those 'Jews' rooted in the schools and synagogues of Tiberias and Tsevat, to say nothing about the Jews of Acco, of Byblos, and of the diaspora throughout the Roman empire?

And, lest we be distracted by this question, what were the non-rabbinic components of the complex region of the Syrian fringe in the Greco-Roman period? Are they to be understood as non-Jewish, anachronistically identifying Judaism as a product of the later Mishnah? To rephrase Keith Whitelam's question: what lost historical societies does the Bible give voice to? Is it itself the anonymous voice of an entire region's intellectual tradition, hidden behind its own creation?

Conclusion

If we will have a critical history, we must deal with the anachronisms we have created. Are the biblical books, themselves, a product of ancient Judaism? Is the continuity between the Bible and Judaism reflective of a chronologically linear development, or is it an aspect of rationalistic anachronism, ideologically motivated: a continuity asserted—like that of Christianity's claim of the *New Testament* and the *Septuaginta*—by theological necessity? Historically, the Bible and the books which make it up are products of the south Levant's worldview: their tradents were those who emerged in the course of the first, or, perhaps better, early second century CE as Samaritans, Jews and Christians; they were both Greeks and Hebrews; both indigenous and people of the diaspora. While all would identify their own heritage with the land 'of the Jews', this was a religious assertion of faith, not a statement of historical fact. Just such associations to Judaism were created in Egypt, in Babylon and in all of the great cities of the Greco-Roman world.

      If I might be allowed a closing remark: after Jerusalem was destroyed by Roman troops in 70 CE, people picked up their lives and continued, and did so again after Bar Kochba's revolt in the second century. When the vast majority of the population of Palestine and Syria became Christian during the Byzantine period, no vast numbers were driven out. Though monophysites were driven eastwards ideologically, the indigenous population continued with a transformed understanding of itself and its religion. Similarly, in the seventh century, when the vast majority of the population of Palestine and Syria became Muslim, few were driven from the land. Though many churches and synagogues became mosques, the indigenous population continued with a transformed understanding of itself and its religion.

3

THE MORAL PROBLEM OF THE LAND TRADITIONS OF THE BIBLE

Michael Prior

The Bible narrates God's promise of the land of Canaan to Abraham and his posterity, and to Moses and his fellow escapees from Egypt. The conquest and settlement of the land are recounted in the Books of Joshua and Judges. These traditions are of considerable scholastic interest, and have implications for our understanding of God, and his relation to the people of Israel, to non-Israelites such as the Canaanites, and, by extension, to all other peoples. Before considering the implications, however, let us review the biblical record of the promise and possession of the land, firstly the narrative of the promise and preparation (the Books of Genesis, Exodus, Leviticus, Numbers and Deuteronomy), and then that of the conquest-settlement (the Books of Joshua and Judges). The moral problem posed by these texts when read at face value will be seen in its starkness.

The Land Traditions of the Bible

The Land Traditions of Genesis-Deuteronomy

In the biblical narrative Yahweh promised the land of Canaan to Abraham and his descendants:

> Abram passed through the land to the place at Schechem,
> to the oak of Moreh. At that time the Canaanites were in
> the land. Then Yahweh appeared to Abram, and said, 'To
> your descendants I will give this land' (Genesis 12.6-7).

With divine approval, Abram moved his tent and came to dwell
by the oaks of Mamre at Hebron, where he built an altar to Yahweh
(Genesis 13.18), and Yahweh made a covenant with Abram/Abraham,
saying,

> To your descendants I give this land, from the river of
> Egypt to the great river, the river Euphrates, the land of the
> Kenites, the Kenizzites, the Kadmonites, the Hittites, the
> Perizzites, the Rephaim, the Amorites, the Canaanites, the
> Girgashites, and the Jebusites (Genesis 15.18-21).

Subsequently, the promise is made to Isaac also (Genesis
26.3-4), and, to guarantee the inheritance, Isaac prayed that the promise
to Abraham would be fulfilled in Jacob (Genesis 28.4; see also 28.13-
15; 35.12). In the final verses of the book, Joseph dying in Egypt said
to his brothers,

> God will surely come to you, and bring you up out of this
> land to the land that he swore to Abraham, to Isaac, and to
> Jacob (Genesis 50.24).

Between the exodus from Egypt (Exodus 1.1-15.21) and the
settlement in Canaan there is the encounter between Yahweh and Moses
on Mount Sinai (Exodus 19.1-40.38). Yahweh gives all that an ancient
people in transition requires, a leader, an identity and a promise of a
future resting place. Yahweh confirms Moses as the leader and speeds
the people on their way to possess the land of Canaan.

The Exodus theme has had a vital influence on later biblical
writers, and in both Jewish and Christian circles symbolizes God's
deliverance of those in bondage:

I have come down to deliver them from the Egyptians, and
to bring them up out of that land to a good and broad land,
a land flowing with milk and honey, to the country of the
Canaanites, the Hittites, the Amorites, the Perizzites, the
Hivites, and the Jebusites' (Exodus 3.8; see also 6.6-8).

Moses' Song of Victory after the crossing of the Red Sea
included reference to the consternation which the destruction of the
Egyptians brought on the inhabitants of Philistia, the chiefs of Edom,
the leaders of Moab, and all the inhabitants of Canaan (Exodus 15.1-
16). Already the Israelites are virtually settled (Exodus 15.17-19).
Exodus 20 deals with the words Yahweh spoke to Moses, and Chapters
21-23 detail the ordinances, including those befitting a settled people,
including,

'When my angel goes in front of you, and brings you to the
Amorites, the Hittites, the Perizzites, the Canaanites, the
Hivites, and the Jebusites, and I blot them out, you shall
not bow down to their gods, or worship them, or follow
their practices, but you shall utterly demolish them and
break their pillars in pieces' (Exodus 23.23-24).

Their warrior god surely will be with them to drive out 'all your
enemies' (Exodus 23.27-33; 33.1-3). Nevertheless, despite the
widespread slaughter of the indigenes, we find the command not to
oppress a resident alien (Exodus 22.21; 23.9). Yahweh promised to
perform marvels for the people, and demanded uncompromising
loyalty, and separation from the Amorites, the Canaanites, the Hittites,
the Perizzites, the Hivites, and the Jebusites (Exodus 34.11-15; see also
34.24).

The gift of the land of Canaan is reiterated in the Book of
Leviticus (Leviticus 14.34), and Yahweh insists on the observance of his
statutes, rather than of those of Egypt or Canaan (Leviticus 18.1-5).
Adherence to the laws of purity is required to ensure residence in the
land (Leviticus 18). Because of their abuses the inhabitants of Canaan
would be vomited out, as would the Israelites also should they commit
abominations, rather than observe Yahweh's statutes (Leviticus 18.24-
30). The conditions for continuing to reside in the land, and for the

separateness of the people are reiterated (Leviticus 20.22-27). Chapter 26 outlines the blessings which will befall the people if they carry out what Yahweh requires: fertility of the soil, peace, victory over enemies, abundant offspring, and the assurance of Yahweh's presence (26.3-13). Disobedience will be rewarded by sevenfold punishment (Leviticus 26.11-39), dispersion and exile (Leviticus 26.32-39). But even in the land of exile, Yahweh will not spurn them nor break his covenant (Leviticus 26.44-46).

The Book of Numbers is organised around three phases of the wandering in the wilderness: the organisation of the community before its departure from Sinai (Numbers 1.1-10.10); the march through the desert from Sinai to the Plains of Moab (Numbers 10.11-21.35); and the preparation for entry into the Promised Land from the Plains of Moab (Numbers 22.1-36.13). No less than 603,550 males from twenty years old and upward (Numbers 1.45-46), and 8,580 Levites would set out (Numbers 4.48). After ensuring the purity of the camp and the community (chaps. 5-6), and performing the rites for the departure (Numbers 7.1-10.10), they march through the desert in stages, as in a liturgical procession, punctuated by moaning, and nostalgia for life in Egypt, from Sinai to the Desert of Paran (Numbers 10.11-12.16) to the threshold of the Promised Land (Numbers 13.1-15.41). The scouts who were sent out reported that the people who lived in the land were strong, and the towns were fortified and very large (Numbers 13.27-29). Nevertheless, Israel made a vow to Yahweh that they would utterly destroy the towns (Numbers 21.1-3). After King Sihon of the Amorites refused free passage, Israel put his troops to the sword, and took his land (Numbers 21.21-24). King Og of Bashan met a similar fate (Numbers 21.34-35).

Yahweh appointed Joshua to succeed Moses (Numbers 27). Chapter 31 brings us back to the war against the Midianites, the killing of every male and of the five kings of Midian. The Israelites captured the women of Midian and their little ones, took all their cattle, burned all their towns and encampments, retaining all the booty, both people and animals. Moses was particularly aggrieved that they allowed the women to live (Numbers 31.8-16). He ordered the killing of every male child, and every woman who had slept with a man. The young girls who z31.18). Then they were to return to the more serious matters of religion, purifying themselves and their garments (Numbers 31.19-20). The booty was divided, and due offerings were made to Yahweh. In the plains of Moab by the Jordan at Jericho, Yahweh spoke to Moses, saying

> Speak to the Israelites, and say to them: 'When you cross
> over the Jordan into the land of Canaan, you shall drive out
> all the inhabitants of the land from before you, destroy all
> their figured stones, destroy all their cast images, and
> demolish all their high places. You shall take possession of
> the land and settle in it, for I have given you the land to
> possess ... But if you do not drive out the inhabitants of
> the land from before you, then those whom you let remain
> shall be as barbs in your eyes and thorns in your sides;
> they shall trouble you in the land where you are settling.
> And I will do to you as I thought to do to them' (Numbers
> 33.50-56).

One of the distinctive emphases of the Book of Deuteronomy is the connection between the people and the land. Although it is hailed as the most theological book of the Old Testament, and advocates an utopian society in which the disadvantaged (the widows, orphans and aliens) are dealt with justly (Lohfink 1996), its treatment of the land and its indigenous inhabitants poses a moral problematic. The book continues the theme of the promise of the land to Abraham, to Isaac, and to Jacob, and their descendants (Deuteronomy 1.6-8). The people were not to be intimidated by the fortified cities, because, 'Yahweh your God who goes before you will himself fight for you, just as he did in Egypt ...' (Deuteronomy 1.30-31).

After Sihon the Amorite King of Heshbon refused passage to the Israelites, Yahweh gave him over to them. They captured and utterly destroyed all the cities, killing all the men, women, and children (Deuteronomy 2.33-34). The fate of Og, King of Bashan was no better (Deuteronomy 3.3). The centrality of observing the Law is again emphasized. After the *Shema* we read,

> And when the Lord your God brings you into the land
> which he swore to your fathers, to Abraham, to Isaac, and
> to Jacob, to give you, with great and goodly cities, which
> you did not build, and houses full of all good things, which
> you did not fill, and cisterns hewn out, which you did not
> hew, and vineyards and olive trees, which you did not

plant, and when you eat and are full, then take heed lest you forget the Lord ... You shall fear the Lord your God; ... lest the anger of the Lord your God be kindled against you, and he destroy you from off the face of the earth (Deuteronomy 6.10-15; see also 6.18-19).

Yahweh's role in the conquest would be vital:

When Yahweh your God brings you into the land that you are about to enter and occupy, and he clears away many nations before you—the Hittites, the Girgashites, the Amorites, the Canaanites, the Perizzites, the Hivites, and the Jebusites, seven nations mightier and more numerous than you—and when Yahweh your God gives them over to you and you defeat them, then you must utterly destroy them. Make no covenant with them and show them no mercy. Do not intermarry with them ... for that would turn away your children from following me, to serve other gods. Then the anger of Yahweh would be kindled against you, and he would destroy you quickly ... Break down their altars, smash their pillars, hew down their sacred poles, and burn their idols with fire. For you are a people holy to Yahweh your God; Yahweh your God has chosen you out of all the peoples on earth to be his people, his treasured possession ... It was because Yahweh loved you ... that Yahweh has brought you out with a mighty hand, and redeemed you from the house of slavery, from the hand of Pharaoh king of Egypt ... Therefore, observe diligently the commandment—the statutes, and the ordinances—that I am commanding you today (Deuteronomy 7.1-11; see also 9.1-5; 11.8-9, 23, 31-32).

The territory shall extend from the wilderness to the Lebanon, and from the Euphrates to the Western Sea (Deuteronomy 11.24).

In the rules for the conduct of war (Deuteronomy 20.1-21.14), when a besieged town surrenders, all its inhabitants shall serve at forced labour; if not, the Israelites shall kill all its males, and take as booty the women, the children, livestock, and everything else in the town (Deuteronomy 20.11-14).

'But as for the towns of these peoples that Yahweh your God is giving you as an inheritance, you must not let anything that breathes remain alive. You shall annihilate them—the Hittites and the Amorites, the Canaanites and the Perizzites, the Hivites and the Jebusites—just as Yahweh your God has commanded, so that they may not teach you to do all the abhorrent things that they do for their gods, and you thus sin against Yahweh your God' (Deuteronomy 20.16-18).

The fruit-bearing trees, however, are to be spared, as is a captive 'beautiful woman whom you desire and want to marry' (Deuteronomy 21.11).

The two ways are put clearly before the people: if they obey the commandments of Yahweh they shall thrive in the land; if not, they shall not live long in the land (Deuteronomy 30.15-20; 32.46-47). The remainder of the book deals with the Last Will and Testament of Moses, and his commissioning of Joshua, who would lead the people across the Jordan (Deuteronomy 31.3-6). Before he was to die, Moses ascended Mount Nebo at Yahweh's command, to be given a view of the land from a distance (Deuteronomy 32.52). The book ends with Moses' sight of the Promised Land (Deuteronomy 34.1-3). Then Moses died and 'was buried in a valley in the land of Moab, opposite Beth-peor, but no one knows his burial place to this day' (v. 6). Joshua was full of the spirit of wisdom, because Moses had laid his hands on him. Although Moses was unequalled in his deeds, he left a worthy successor (Deuteronomy 34.4-12).

The Land in the Books of Joshua and Judges

Joshua is presented as the divinely-chosen and worthy successor of Moses, who is destined to complete his work (Joshua 1). The first part (2.1-12.24) describes in epic style the conquest of the land, concentrating on the capture of a few key cities, and their treatment in accordance with the laws of the Holy War. Then we have the division of the land (13.1-21.45), followed by an appendix (22.1-24.33).

The spies Joshua sent to Jericho reported back that all the inhabitants of the land melted in fear before them (Joshua 1.24). The crossing of the Jordan is described in Joshua 3.1-5.1, followed by the ceremonies at Gilgal (Joshua 5.2-12), and the destruction of Jericho (Joshua 5.13-6.27). After the seventh (ritual) procession of the Ark around the walls of the city on the seventh day, the wall fell down flat at the sound of the trumpets and the great shout (Joshua 6.20). The city and all that was in it, with the exception of Rahab and her house, would be devoted to Yahweh for destruction (*herem*) (Joshua 6.17). The slaughter of all the men and women, oxen, sheep, and donkeys, and the burning of the city followed, sparing only the silver and gold, etc., for the treasury of the house of Yahweh, as well as Rahab's family. Joshua pronounced a curse on anyone who tries to rebuild Jericho (Joshua 6.21-27).

The marauding party moved on to Ai at Yahweh's command, to do to it what was done to Jericho: no one of the twelve thousand inhabitants survived or escaped, and Joshua burned it, and made it forever a heap of ruins, 'as it is to this day' (Joshua 8.2, 19-29). The liturgical *Te Deum* and reading of the Law followed in style, with one choir on Mount Gerizim and the other on Mount Ebal (Joshua 8.30-35). The ravaging troops of Joshua and Israel were to be met with a concerted defence of the Hittites, the Amorites, the Canaanites, the Perizzites, the Hivites, and the Jebusites (Joshua 9.1-2). But the inhabitants of Gibeon were to be spared the conditions of the ban (*herem*), and were destined to become 'hewers of wood and drawers of water for all the congregation' (Joshua 9.21, 23, 27). The elders complained at this lapse in fidelity to the mandate to destroy all the inhabitants of the land (Joshua 9.24).

The next two chapters give details of the shift in the theatre of marauding. Chapter 10 describes the campaign in the south, and chapter 11 that in the north, in each case, assuring the rigorous enforcement of the ban (*herem*). Chapter 10 describes how five kings made war against the Gibeonites who appealed to Joshua, who inflicted a great slaughter on the kings' forces at Gibeon. Later, Joshua struck down the five kings who had been hiding in the cave at Makkedah, and put them to death. In conformity with the rules of the Holy War, Joshua took Makkedah and utterly destroyed every person in it (Joshua 10.28). A similar fate befell Libnah, Lachish, Eglon, Hebron, and Debir (Joshua 10.29-39). The author summarises Joshua's destruction of everything that breathed, from Kadesh-barnea to Gaza and so on, as Yahweh commanded (Joshua 10. 40-43).

Chapter 11 describes the northern campaign, with the literary account showing signs of a conscious parallel with chapter 10. The coalition between the kings of the northern hill country, and in the Arabah, and in the lowland, the Canaanites in the east and the west, the Amorites, the Hittites, the Perizzites, and the Jebusites, and the Hivites (Joshua 11.1-3) was no match for Joshua, with Yahweh on his side. Israel struck them down, until they had left no one remaining (Joshua 11.7-9). The reader is given a résumé of the military campaign. Joshua took all the land, utterly destroying its inhabitants (Joshua 11.16-23). Chapter 12 gives a full list of the kings defeated, and the lands conquered, firstly under Moses on the east side of the Jordan (Joshua 12.1-6), and then on the west (Joshua 12.7-24). The whole achievement is summed up in that Yahweh gave to Israel all the land that he swore to their ancestors that he would give them (Joshua 21.43-45).

The picture in the Book of Judges is considerably different from that recorded in the Book of Joshua. Whereas the Book of Joshua gives details of the conquest in a series of 'punctiliar', efficient military activities, the Book of Judges sees it as a more complex and gradual phenomenon, punctuated by partial success and failure.

The Land in other Books of the Bible

The theme of land recurs in several traditions within the Bible. However, the evidence that these traditions were in circulation before the period of the Babylonian exile (586 BC) is meagre. In the eighth-century Judean prophets, Isaiah and Micah, we read only of the Midian story (Isaiah 10.26). In the northern kingdom, we have a reference to the Amorites in Amos 2.10, and a possible reference to the outrage at Gibeah in Hosea 9.9. With respect to the celebration of the occupation of the land within the cultic life of the community, there is little that one would have to put earlier than the period of the exile (586-538 BC). While Psalm 65.9-13 lauds Yahweh for his benevolence towards the land in general, Psalm 78:54-55 does so for his specific care of the Israelites:

> And he brought them to his holy hill, to the mountain that his right hand had won. He drove out nations before them; he apportioned them for a possession and settled the tribes of Israel in their tents.

This theme is reiterated in other psalms:

You brought a vine out of Egypt; you drove out the nations and planted it (Psalm 80.8).

So he brought his people out with joy, his chosen ones with singing. He gave them the lands of the nations, and they took possession of the wealth of the peoples (Psalm 105.43-44).

However, the details of the conquest are inconsiderable. Psalm 114 does refer to the stopping of the flow of the Jordan, and Psalms 78.54-66 and 81.11-12 refer to the disobedience of Israel. However, there is no reason to insist that these compositions pre-date the exile, or that they were not derived from the books of Joshua and Judges.

There is a notable lack of evidence, therefore, for the popularity of the conquest and settlement traditions prior to the period of the exile. In that period, they assume an importance in both Jeremiah and Ezekiel. However, neither in Jeremiah nor Ezekiel is there specific reference to the land having been conquered by Joshua and the Judges. Moreover, there are no clear allusions to the conquest and settlement traditions in Isaiah 40-55 or in the post-exilic prophets. It is remarkable that, with the exception of their importance in the texts discussed above, the conquest and settlement traditions occupy such an insignificant place within the Bible. Yet, however late the traditions, the narratives pose moral problems.

The Moral Problem of the Biblical Land Traditions

The moral problematic is exacerbated by the fact that the traditions belong within a literature which enjoys unique authority within both Synagogue and Church. In the estimation of Jews, the *Torah* emanates from heaven, and a punctilious observance of its laws is the supreme religious duty (Schürer 1979: 314). The *Torah*, in such an interpretation, must be accepted in its totality, and in all its parts. The Bible enjoys a corresponding authority in the Church as the Word of God.

Manifestly, the biblical narrative poses a fundamental moral problem for anyone who takes it at face value. In the narrative, the

Hebrew slaves who left Egypt invaded a land already occupied, and engaged in systematic pillage and killing. What distinguishes the biblical account, whether through the *Blitzkrieg* mode represented in the Book of Joshua, or the more gradual one reflected in the Book of Judges, is that it is presented as having not only divine approval, but as being mandated by the divinity. In the Book of Joshua, in particular, the Israelites killed in conformity with the directives of God. This presentation of God as requiring the destruction of others poses problems for anyone who presumes that the conduct of an ethical God will not fall lower than decent, secular behaviour.

The commandment that, 'You shall devour all the peoples that Yahweh your God is giving over to you, showing them no pity' (Deuteronomy 7.16) is seen in a new light, when one recalls how such texts were used in support of colonialism in several regions and periods, in which the native peoples were the counterparts of the Hittites, the Girgashites, etc.[1] Were it not for their religious provenance, such biblical sentiments would be regarded as incitements to racial hatred. *Prima facie,* judged by the standards of ethics and human rights to which our society has become accustomed, the first six books of the Hebrew Bible reflect some ethnocentric, racist and xenophobic sentiments, which appear to receive the highest possible legitimacy in the form of divine approval. On moral grounds, one is forced to question whether the *Torah* continues to provide divine legitimacy for the occupation of other people's land, and the virtual annihilation of the indigenes. G E M de Ste Croix notes the unprecedented character of these traditions of divinely mandated ferocity, which are relayed not by hostile sources but by the very literature they themselves regard as sacred (in Said 1988: 166).

The Israeli socio-psychologist, Georges R Tamarin surveyed the presence of prejudices in the ideology of Israeli youth, and the effect of

---

[1] In my *The Bible and Colonialism: A Moral Critique* (1997) I focus on three different regions and periods, in which each colonialist ideology gained the support of a distinctive religious ideology: the invasion of Latin America in the fifteenth century, the Dutch incursion into the Cape Colony of southern Africa in 1652, and its sequel in the nineteenth and twentieth centuries, and Zionist settler-colonialism of Palestine in this century. Earlier, while the Crusader Templars ate their meals in silence they enjoyed public readings from the Bible, with special emphasis on the Books of Joshua and the Maccabees. All found inspiration in the ferocious exploits of Judas, his brothers and their war-bands in reconquering the Holy Land from cruel infidels (Seward 1995: 32).

an uncritical teaching of the Bible on the propensity for forming prejudices. He was particularly anxious to evaluate the degree to which uncritical teaching of notions of the 'chosen people', the superiority of monotheistic religion, and the study of acts of genocide carried out by biblical heroes contributed to the development of prejudice. He chose the Book of Joshua (the capture of Jericho, Joshua 6.20-21, and of Makkedah, Joshua 10.28-32) because of its special position in the Israeli educational system, both as national history and as one of the cornerstones of Israel's national mythology. Tamarin's study showed the existence of a highly prejudiced attitude among a considerable number of the respondents, justifying discriminatory tendencies, and interpreted this result as proving unequivocally the influence of chauvinism and nationalist-religious prejudices on moral judgement (1973: 187-88). He concluded that,

> The uncritical teaching of the Bible—to students too young—even if not taught explicitly as a sacred text, but as national history or in a quasi-neutral atmosphere concerning the real or mythological character of its content, no doubt profoundly affects the genesis of prejudices ... even among non-religious students, in accentuating the negative-hostile character of the strangers (1973: 189).

Tamarin concluded that the findings were a severe indictment of the Israeli educational system, and an invitation to those responsible to learn from them. His research brought him unsought and unexpected notoriety and led to his losing his professorship in Tel Aviv University. In a letter to the senate of the university he wrote that he had never dreamt that he would become the last victim of Joshua's conquest of Jericho (1973: 190).

The Bible, Peace and Colonialism

Discussion among biblical scholars and theologians on the subject of the settlement of the children of Israel in Canaan in antiquity is distinguished by its neglect of consideration for the inhabitants of the region prior to those occupations, even though the biblical paradigm has been used to sanction the British conquest of North America, Ireland and Australia, the Dutch conquest of South Africa, the Prussian conquest of Poland, and the Zionist conquest of Palestine. The absence of concern for 'the natives' reflects the deeply ingrained Eurocentric, colonialist prejudice which characterises virtually all historiography, as well as the discipline of biblical studies (see Whitelam 1996 *passim*).

Nevertheless, liberation theologians from virtually every region (Latin America, South Africa, South Korea, the Philippines, etc.) have appropriated the Exodus story in their long and tortuous struggle against colonialism, imperialism and dictatorship. Readers of the biblical narrative are easily impressed and consoled by that story's capacity to lift the spirits of the oppressed. However, one's perspective on the Exodus story takes on a different complexion when read with the eyes of the 'Canaanites', that is, of any of several different cultures, which have been victims of a colonialism fired by religious imperialism, whether of the Indians in North or Latin America, the Maoris in New Zealand, the Aborigines in Australia, the Khoikhoi and San in southern Africa, or, the Palestinians in Palestine.

The Palestinian liberation theologian, Canon Naim Ateek poses the problematic in a striking fashion, since in his region, above all others, the applicability of the Exodus paradigm appears most natural.

> Before the creation of the State (of Israel), the Old Testament was considered to be an essential part of Christian Scripture, pointing and witnessing to Jesus. Since the creation of the State, some Jewish and Christian interpreters have read the Old Testament largely as a Zionist text to such an extent that it has become almost repugnant to Palestinian Christians … The fundamental question of many Christians, whether uttered or not, is: 'How can the Old Testament be the Word of God in the light of the Palestinian Christians' experience with its use to support Zionism?' (Ateek 1991: 283).

The Bible, commonly looked to as the supreme source-book of liberation, has functioned as a charter for oppression, both in the past and the present. Understandably, the symbiotic relationship between the political and religious discourses is most focused in the case of Zionism and Palestine. If other peoples can apply the biblical paradigm of conquest and plunder by recourse to claims to analogous 'rights', the rights of Jews are accorded canonical and unique status and are warmly supported in the West. The religious-political link was illustrated dramatically on 13 September 1993, when President Clinton introduced Prime Minister Rabin and President Arafat on the White House lawn. He announced to the world that both people pledged themselves to a shared future, 'shaped by the values of the *Torah,* the Koran, and the Bible'. According to a report in the *Washington Post,* the President, fearing that his speech required more work, had not been able to sleep on the night before the signing. He woke at 3.00 a.m., and reread the entire Book of Joshua and portions of the New Testament (Prior 1994: 20). His mode of address later in the day was a mixture of Bible-based exhortation in the Baptist tradition, and shrewd political manoeuvring. The late Premier Rabin's speech also referred to the Bible. However, in the light of history one must question whether *the values of the Torah, the Koran, and the Bible* can be relied upon to promote justice and peace, and underpin the imperatives of human rights.

When Dr Baruch Goldstein, a graduate of the most prestigious *yeshiva* in the USA, massacred twenty-nine worshippers in the Ibrahimi Mosque in Hebron (25 February 1994), there was widespread revulsion. Even advocates of the *Torah-from-Heaven* expressed shock at the unspeakably evil act of violence against those engaged in worship. Nevertheless, one asks what distinguishes this kind of behaviour from that presented as divinely mandated in some of the traditions of the *Torah,* and from the appropriation of those traditions by different forms of colonialism and imperialism? One wonders to what extent the Book of Deuteronomy, the Book of Joshua, and, in particular, the Book of Esther, the prescribed reading for the feast of Purim which occurred on that day, may have contributed to the world view of Dr Goldstein. His actions were supported by some Zionists who lean heavily on a literalist reading of the biblical text (see Prior 1994).

Sadly, Prime Minister Rabin left this particularly loathsome form of applied biblical hermeneutics unchecked. By a sad irony, Rabin himself was gunned down at a Tel Aviv Peace Rally on 4 November 1995. In the first hearing of his case, Yigal Amir explained that he derived his motivation from *halakhah.* British Chief Rabbi Sacks invited the Orthodox rabbinate to question whether they were really teaching Jewish values: the *Torah* was given, 'not to wreak vengeance, but to create kindness, compassion and peace.' He went on to stress that it is 'people of religious conviction, who must most forcibly defend the democratic process. We must absolutely—as a matter of Jewish principle—reject utterly the language of hate' (*Jewish Chronicle,* 10 November 1995, p. 56). Whether Rabbi Sacks owes more to the ideals of Enlightenment philosophy, than to that particular form of Orthodox Judaism which reads the biblical text in a literalist way, is not clear.

With respect to biblical hermeneutics, Goldstein and Amir, and more recently, Israeli soldier Noam Friedman who fired indiscriminately at Palestinians in Hebron on New Year's Day 1997, are merely the tip of the iceberg of literalism, which justifies outrages on the basis of an alleged divine mandate. Constant exposure to a literalist interpretation of the *Torah,* whether in the curriculum of Israeli schools, or through some of the many schools of biblical and talmudic learning avoids with difficulty descent into attitudes of racism, xenophobia and militarism (see Newman, ed. 1985). Moreover, there is abundant evidence, especially in traditions of imperialist colonialism emanating from so-called Christian countries, for appeal to sacred writings to justify inhumane behaviour.

Reading the Bible with the Eyes of Canaanites

Contemporary liberation theologies look to the Bible for their underpinning. It is not difficult to discern a range of themes which fit the concept of liberation very comfortably (e.g., liberation from oppression in Egypt, Babylon, etc.). However, does not a consistent reading of the biblical text require the liberating God of the Exodus to become the oppressive God of the occupation of Canaan? The problem is held in sharp relief in the comment of a North American Indian:

> The obvious characters for Native Americans to identify with are the Canaanites, the people who already lived in the promised land ... I read the Exodus stories with Canaanite eyes (Warrior 1991: 289).

The black people of South Africa recognise the central position which the Bible occupied in their colonisation, national oppression and exploitation. Paradoxically, as converts to Christianity, the religion of their conquerors, they embraced the Bible, the text book of their exploitation. However, accordingly as they encounter the Bible being used in support of unjust causes they realise that the book itself is a serious problem for people in search of freedom. Many young South African blacks consider the Bible to be an oppressive document by its very nature and its very core, and even call for its displacement.

Religious and theological comment on contemporary developments in Palestine is substantial, but that reflecting a moral sensitivity to the underside of the establishment of the Jewish State of Israel, namely the disruption of the indigenous Arab population of Palestine is modest. Biblically- and theologically-based discussion concerning this region is singularly deficient in its interest in those issues with which human rights and humanitarian bodies concern themselves. This is not only surprising but alarming, since biblical scholars and theologians in virtually every other arena inform their discussions with a sensitivity to the victims of oppression. Until recently both Jewish and Christian scholars of the Bible have neglected the theme of the land. The view that the Bible provides the title-deed for the establishment of the modern state of Israel, and for its policies since 1948 is so pervasive, not only in both Christian Zionist and Jewish Zionist circles but even within mainstream Christian theology and university biblical studies, that the very attempt to discuss the issue is sure to encounter opposition.

Many theologians sensitive to issues of human rights, especially those whose traditions depend heavily on the Bible face a dilemma. While they revere the sacred text, they see how it has been used as an instrument of oppression. They seek refuge in the view that it is the mis-use of the Bible, rather than the text of the Bible itself which is the problem. The blame is shifted from the non-problematic biblical text to the perverse predispositions of the biblical interpreter. This 'solution' evades the problem. Examples from the past and the present indicate the pervasiveness, the persistence and the moral seriousness of the question. Several traditions within the Bible lend themselves to oppressive interpretations and applications, precisely because of their inherently oppressive nature.

Whereas the Bible was used as a justification for, and, paradoxically, as a condemnation of Spanish and Portuguese colonialism as that enterprise was in process of development in the medieval period, in the case of Afrikaner colonialism and nationalism the Exodus-settlement paradigm was appealed to *post factum* as a justifying device for colonialism, but as an ever-present support for *separate development*. And no less paradoxically than in the case of Spanish and Portuguese colonialism, the rejection of oppression as an acceptable ideology was greatly assisted by appeal to the Bible (see Prior 1997: 48-105). Virtually all historians working on the nineteenth century now reject the still commonly held view that the Afrikaners who embarked on the Great Trek (c. 1836) considered themselves to be sanctioned to dispossess the indigenous Black population, after the fashion of the Israelites whom the biblical accounts present as having been mandated by the divinity to cleanse Canaan of its population.

In South African society in which there was a coalition between religion and the state, religion provided a transcendent referent for the exercise of political sovereignty, and the prevailing Dutch Reformed theology underpinned *apartheid*. Biblical scholars hesitate to accept their responsibility. While Deist, for example, points up the problem which the biblical text presents to a reader, he is reluctant to concede that the Book of Deuteronomy is a dangerous book in itself, since it predicates racist, xenophobic and militaristic tendencies as deriving from the will of God. He deals with the problem by exonerating the biblical authors and by ascribing to the reader alone any morally dubious pre-dispositions (Deist 1994: 28-29). Reflecting the Black experience, however, Mofokeng goes to the heart of the matter. Black people of South Africa point to three dialectically related realities:

> They show the central position which the Bible occupied in the ongoing process of colonization, national oppression and exploitation. They also confess the incomprehensible paradox of being colonised by a Christian people and yet being converted to their religion and accepting the Bible, their ideological instrument of colonization, oppression and exploitation. Thirdly, they express a historic commitment that is accepted solemnly by one generation and passed onto another—a commitment to terminate exploitation of humans by other humans (Mofokeng 1988: 34).

He goes on,

> When Black Christians see all these conservative and
> reactionary efforts and hear the Bible being quoted in
> support of reactionary causes they realise that the Bible
> itself is a serious problem to people who want to be free
> (1988: 37).

The Bible and Zionist Colonialism

From its conception in the late 1890s to its implementation since,
Zionism, although distinctive in some critical respects, was a political
ideology sharing much in common with nineteenth-century European
nationalisms and colonialisms. In line with prevailing European racisms
which predicated inferiority of all native peoples, Zionism determined
to improve the lot of international Jewry at the expense of the
indigenous population of Palestine. To achieve success, its programme
required the support of major international powers, initially of Britain,
and more recently of the United States. The existence of a friendly state
in the strategically important Middle East would be of considerable
value to the foreign policy interests of first Britain, and then the USA.

Although the Zionist conquest of Palestine has many precedents
(e.g., the European settlement in North America, or the British one in
Australia and New Zealand), it had several unique features. The
displacement took place within decades rather than two or three
centuries. Secondly, the Zionist colonisation took place after the heyday
of European colonisation, and at a time when the European colonising
nations were beginning to respect the right to self-determination of
indigenous populations, and when the very notion of colonisation was
beginning to break down. Thirdly, although the Zionist colonisation has
taken place in an age of mass communications, until recently it has
managed to portray itself as an innocent victim reaping its just rewards.
But, most distinctively, the Zionist colonial enterprise has widespread
religious support, Christian as well as Jewish, and in some theological
and religious circles is viewed as being consistent with biblical
prophecy, or at least being no more than what the Jewish people deserve
in virtue of the promises of God outlined in the Bible.

Much of the ideological thrust in Zionism derives from a
literalist interpretation of the biblical witness to land and of some of its
messianic texts, with scant attention to the rights of the indigenes.

However, as an agent of legitimacy in international law, the Zionist appeal to the Bible for legitimation of its claims to *Eretz Israel* is not much more compelling that if the Portuguese and Spanish governments today, in a bid to reclaim the lands of the New World, presented to the United Nations the Bulls of Popes Nicholas V and Alexander VI which also claimed divine authority. In any case, no claim can be accorded an absolute status, but must be weighed up in conjunction with the claims of others.

With respect to the indigenous non-Jews of Palestine, one detects a disjuncture between the cynical ideals of the preamble to Israel's Declaration of Independence (14 May 1948) and the reality of the enterprise:

> The State of Israel will ... foster the development of the country for the benefit of all its inhabitants: it will be based on freedom, justice and peace as envisaged by the prophets of Israel. It will ensure complete equality of social and political rights to all its inhabitants irrespective of religion, conscience, language, education, and culture; it will safeguard the Holy places of all religions and it will be faithful to the principles of the charter of the United Nations.

It would appear in some formulations of the Zionist conquest that the indigenes should appreciate their passive path to redemption, via the Jewish homecoming. There is no shortage of utopian idealisations of the promise of God's gift of land to the children of Israel: 'The union of people and land is intended to contribute to the perfecting of the world in order to become the Kingdom of God' (Buber 1973: 47). Whereas other nations who dispossessed indigenous people can legitimately be accused of robbery,

> Their charge against Israel is totally unjust for it acted under authority and in the confident knowledge of its authorization ... No other people has ever heard and accepted the command from heaven as did the people of Israel ... So long as it sincerely carried out the command it was in the right and is in the right in so far as it still carries it out. Its unique relationship to its land must be

> seen in this light … Where a command and a faith are
> present, in certain historical situations conquest need not
> be robbery (Buber 1973: 146).

For André Neher too, the land Palestine holds the key to Jewish existence. He writes of a 'geo-theology' and its charm, and supports the view that *aliyah* will speed up the redemption of the whole world, and the coming of the Messiah (1992: 22-23). But the spiritual and moral tenets of the *Torah* must be obeyed, because, otherwise the land will vomit Israel forth, as it previously vomited the Canaanites, 'to whom God had confided it in a moment of hasty imprudence' (Neher 1992: 20). The State of Israel is the agent of mass reconciliation: of Jews, Christians and Muslims; of the sacred and the profane; and of Jews who differ in their messianic expectations (1992: 27-29). The reconciliatory impact of the return-to-Zion enterprise does not appear quite so sanguine from my perspective as I write, overlooking the 'border' check-point between Bethlehem and Jerusalem, and surrounded by so many signs of colonial plunder, as well as witnessing the daily humiliation of the indigenous population which is made to experience alienation and exile within its own homeland.

There is no doubt that the Jewish religious establishment, although late in embracing Zionism, today virtually fully supports its achievement. For many religious Jews, the State of Israel is 'the most powerful collective expression' of Jewry, and 'the most significant development in Jewish life since the Holocaust' (Jonathan Sacks, Chief Rabbi of Britain). Moreover, the religious wing is at the forefront of the opposition to political 'compromise' (a euphemism for 'restitution') with the Palestinians, with very few Orthodox rabbis supporting it, and many at the vanguard of its destruction. It is a matter of concern that religious Jews have little regard for the indigenes who have paid the price for the establishment of Israel. But neither did Joshua in the biblical narrative.

The rhetoric of the sacral discourse of the achievement of Zionism is undermined by the reality of the catastrophe for the indigenous population. The establishment of a Jewish state involved the eviction of the majority of the Palestinians, and the destruction of most of their villages, and the continual use of force and state terrorism, wars and military operations. The daily humiliation of the indigenous people and the litany of other atrocities casts a dark cloud over the achievement of the ethnocentric dream of nineteenth century Jewish nationalist colonialists. What is most distressing from a moral and religious perspective is that the major ideological support for Zionist imperialism and the principal obstacle against treating the indigenous people with respect come from religious circles for whom the biblical narratives of land are normative. Already in 1913, the bad behaviour of Zionists towards the Palestinians made Ahad Ha'am fear for the future if Jews ever came to power: 'If this be the "Messiah": I do not wish to see his coming' (in Lehn 1988: 13).

Colonial Stereotypes

Although the practice of settler colonialism is distinctive in each case there are stereotypical attitudes to the indigenous people. Invariably for colonisation to take place, the coloniser had to be technically, materially and militarily more developed than the colonised. By the criteria of the coloniser, these qualities conferred superiority, 'natural' or 'racial', and justified 'the insatiable progress of our race'. The colonisers seldom considered the impact of their enterprise on the indigenous population, and either ignored it, or knew what was best for the natives, and arrogated to themselves the right to be overseers of their destiny, whether in reservations in the USA,[2] *congregaciones* and *aldeias* in Latin America, *Bantustans* in South Africa, or Zones A of the Palestinian National Authority.

Consistent with the practice in virtually all nations and political movements, the historiographers of Zionism and the State of Israel fabricated a history of origins. Having forged a myth of a perennial Jewish longing to abandon the *galut* (exile) and establish a Jews-only state in the ancestral homeland, they posited it as the norm in every generation, even though such an aspiration did not appear in Jewish

---

[2] In the nineteenth century, the USA government adopted a policy of 'population transfer' of hundreds of thousands of Indians from their own land into reservations. Such an act required no further justification than that provided by the obvious superiority of the white man over the Indian. Moreover, any semblance of moral culpability for the action was removed by naming the operation 'The Manifest Destiny'. See Dee Brown's *Bury my Heart at Wounded Knee* (1981), in particular p. 31, for an insight into 'Manifest Destiny'.

circles until the rise of other nationalisms in nineteenth-century Europe. The aspiration to establish a nation state in Palestine made noappearance in Jewish history between the defeat of Bar Kochba's revolt in 135 AD and the advent of nineteenth-century European nationalism. In fact, Jewish longing for the land was akin to the longing for a lost Paradise of Temple ritual. In religious circles, the exceptional nationalistic views of Rabbis Kalischer and Alkalai ran in the face of the Orthodox establishment. Zionism depended on no religious sensitivities, and was consistently opposed by the religious establishment; indeed the major Zionist ideologues despised religion. One should not forge the rich diversity of pre-Zionist Jewry into an inevitable linear progression to one agreed ideology, be it Zionism or some other. The fabricated proto-Zionist myth of the pre-history of political Zionism not only distorts the truth of history, but perverts present-day Jews' perception of themselves, their origins and their destiny.

The amassing of texts from different periods and places, reflecting a certain alienation from the Holy Land and a discomfort in the diaspora, does not amount to evidence of a perennial and ubiquitous persecution of Jews. As the survival of Jews shows, the peril was neither everywhere nor at all times. There were golden ages in the diaspora, as well as dark ones. Indeed in 1950-51, Ben-Gurion felt obliged to sanction the bombing of synagogues and other Jewish buildings in Baghdad to engineer the *aliyah* of Jews from Iraq—an immensely successful campaign, which drove some 105,000 Jews to flee the country with no choice of destination other than Israel, leaving only some 4,000 behind (Shiblak 1986: 127).[3]

Diaspora longing for the land of Israel was invariably linked to Temple worship. However, attachment to the Temple rituals, and the desire to rebuild the Temple and restore its animal sacrifices must take account of realities. The Passover Eve supplement of the Israeli daily newspaper *Ha'aretz* ('The Holy Butcher Shop', 14 April 1995) shocked

---

[3] Agents of the Israeli government spread the fear of antisemitism into the Iraqi Jews by blowing up synagogues (e.g., the Mas'uda Shemtob Synagogue on 14 January 1951), firms owned by Jews (May and June 1951), and other places frequented by Jews, as well as the US Information Centre in Baghdad (March 1951), in order to gain support for the Zionist cause in the US. The bombing campaign, carried out with the personal knowledge of Yigal Allon and David Ben-Gurion, was sustained over a period of time in order to ensure a mass exodus of Iraqi Jews to Israel: 'Every time fears would abate, a new bomb shattered the feeling of security, and the prospect of staying on in Iraq seemed gloomier' (Shiblak 1986: 124).

its readers with its description of how the Temple ritual actually functioned with animal sacrifices, etc. The ritual of priests skinning and dividing the animals, and the stench from the daily burning of hundreds of sheep and bulls as sacrifices, etc. would temper the nostalgia for the earthly Jerusalem that is at the heart of diaspora longing. Pilgrimage to Jerusalem also was motivated by attachment to the site of the Temple. The exclamation, 'Next year in Jerusalem' was in anticipation of a pilgrimage to the site of the Temple, and not a proto-Zionist aspiration to establish a colonial settlement. Spiritual and emotional attachment to the land should not be confused with wishing to live there, and less with the desire to control it politically, especially at the expense of the indigenes. Essentially, pilgrims visit a place and return home.

In their determination to present an unblemished record of the Zionist achievement, the historiographers of Zionism and the State of Israel rewrote not only their history, but the documents upon which such a history were based (see Morris 1995: 56-57). In his sanitised version of the conquest of Arab villages, Ben-Gurion makes no reference to massacres, rapes and expulsions, and presents the massive looting of the towns and villages as the only 'moral shortcoming' of Israeli behaviour (Morris 1995: 56-57). Yosef Weitz 'laundered' the diaries of Yosef Nahmani, removing all reference to massacres in the 'stenographic' records of meetings, and all citations of Nahmani's consistent criticism of the aggressiveness and wanton cruelty of the Haganah, who on orders from their command refused to negotiate with the Arabs, who 'only want peace' (Morris 1995: 54). Morris considers the fabricators of propagandistic Zionist history to be among the most accomplished practitioners of this strange craft of source-doctoring (1995: 44). The aim was to hide things said and done, and to bequeath to posterity only a sanitised version of the past.

One of the most significant effects of a pan-Zionist reading of Jewish history is the reduction of the rich diversity of Jewish historical experience to one kind of ideological drive which emphasises some of the most ignoble and regressive elements of Jewish tradition, namely those which glory in a separation from the nations, and a determination to carve out the destiny of a Jewish state, irrespective of the cost to others. These dispositions which derive from an ethnicist and xenophobic nationalism, and are premised on attitudes of racial dominance and exclusion do not advance the goal of other traditions within Judaism, such as that inviting the Jewish community to be a light to the nations.

This rewriting of Jewish history has gone hand in glove with the myth which propels Zionism, and catapults to the zenith of Jewish aspirations a single phase of its history that is very recent, and one that in all likelihood will not endure. It will not endure, in the same way that tyrannies collapse eventually, usually under the weight of a combination of internal tensions which spring from ideological contradictions, and external ones which will not tolerate or support such oppression indefinitely. Pre-Zionist Judaism deserves to be assessed on its own terms, and the whole of Jewish history must not be allowed to be dominated by the combined forces of nineteenth-century imperialist and colonial-nationalist tendencies and the disaster inflicted on European Jewry by the racist policies of the Third Reich.

Fundamentally, the Jewish claim to return rests with the Bible, since there is no other convincing moral ground supporting it. What most distinguishes the wholesale foundational plunder which Zionism perpetrated on the indigenous Palestinians is the fact that it is generally regarded favourably in the West, and in most theological and religious circles is viewed as being no more than what the Jewish people deserve in virtue of the promises of God outlined in the Bible. The Bible is a *sine qua non* for the provision of alleged moral legitimacy, and without it Zionism is a discourse in the conquest mode, as against a moral one. The Bible read at face value provides not only a moral framework which transposes Jewish claims into a divinely sanctioned legitimacy, but postulates the taking possession of the Promised Land and the forcible expulsion of the indigenous population as the fulfilment of a biblical mandate. One could scarcely imagine that the Messianic Age would open with colonial plunder.

Modern Scholarship and the Biblical Narratives

Twentieth-century biblical scholarship has shifted from viewing much of the biblical narrative as simple history to concentrating on its authors as historiographers, whose reconstruction of the past reflected their own religious and political ideologies. However, no amount of special pleading is sufficient to justify the classification 'history' for the biblical narrative of Israelite origins. *Pace* Brettler's strained attempts to retain the term for much of the biblical narrative (1995: 10-12), no 'didactic history' which 'patterned the past after the present', or even fabricated the past for allegedly honest paraenetic motives should be confused with the discipline of history whose criteria are accuracy and adequacy of portrayal of the past, independently confirmed where possible.[4] History proper must be distinguished from a series of ideologically motivated assertions about the past (see Thompson 1992: 404-405).

Biblical scholarship can include the biblical texts from the Book of Genesis to the Book of Kings within the genre of historiography only by a tortuous expansion of the definition. Such a designation confuses the world of historiography which deals with the true and real past with that of fictional literature which reflects the conceptual world of the author. The material from the Book of Genesis to the Book of Kings, which preserves fragmentary sources emanating from many authors reflecting diverse ideologies and retaining seemingly disharmonious tale variations, does not merit the genre of self-conscious historiography as understood in antiquity or today. The one responsible for transmitting these traditions appears to have been driven by an antiquarian's desire to preserve the diversity of what was old, while giving it a loosely chronological catalogue of a sequence of great periods (see Thompson 1992: 373-78).

The rejection of the historicity of the patriarchal narratives of the Book of Genesis in the seminal works of Thompson (1974) and van Seters (1975) is now part of the scholarly consensus that the narratives do not record events of the patriarchal period, but are retrojections into a past about which the writers knew little, which reflect the authorial intentions at the later period of composition. The narratives of Genesis-Deuteronomy are best understood as common traditions of Judah sometime after 600 BC, and should not be used as historiographical sources for the period before 1000 BC (Lemche 1985: 385-86), and should be used only very rarely for the period of the monarchy itself

---

[4] Brettler argues that the author of the Book of Chronicles wrote a type of 'didactic history', which 'patterned the past after the present', in which what might be learned from the event or pattern, rather than the historicity of the event itself was important. Such a work ought to be read in terms of the meaning which the narrative conveys, rather than as a record of past events (1995: 41). Brettler is at pains to retain the biblical writers within the category of historians. Although the Deuteronomist modified and diverged from his sources radically, and 'fabricated' history, he is excused, because he honestly believed his ideology, and is conceded to be 'writing history like all other historians' (1995: 78).

(Thompson 1992: 95). While ancient Israelite historiographers may not have been much different from the later Jewish rabbis, for whom 'therewas no question more meaningless or boring than the purpose and usefulness of an exact description of what actually transpired' (Moshe David Herr, in Brettler 1995: 2), the questions concerning what, or whether God's promise of land to an Abraham and his descendants actually happened are of critical importance.

Against the background of the virtually unanimous scholarly scepticism concerning the historicity of the patriarchal narratives, it is unacceptable to cleave to the view that God made the promise of progeny and land to Abraham after the fashion indicated in Genesis 15. Literary and historical investigation make it more likely that such promises emanated from within the ideologies of a much later period, perhaps that of the attempt to reconstitute national and religious identity in the wake of the Babylonian exile. Nevertheless, despite their legendary character, both Church and Synagogue continue to treat the patriarchal narratives as though they were a record of what actually happened. The scholarly community for its part evades the problem by contenting itself with studying the texts, rather than the events which lie behind them (see Brettler 1995: 1-2; Neusner 1990: 247).

Much of the scholastic reaction against viewing the Abraham narrative as late and largely legendary is motivated by 'confessional' considerations.[5] This disposition springs from a fear that any deviation from 'historical' truth is a dilution of, and derogation from religious truth, as if history (in the sense of a record of what really happened) were the only literary genre worthy, or even capable of communicating religious truth.[6] It is as if factual history were the only genre which could validate a religious appreciation of the narrative of the call of Abraham and the promise of progeny and land: Christian faith and Jewish belief demand no less. However, an authentic biblical faith must respect the variety of literary forms of the biblical *narrative,* and

---

[5] 'Without Abraham, a major block in the foundations of both Judaism and Christianity is lost; a fictional Abraham ... could supply no rational evidence for faith ... Inasmuch as the Bible claims uniqueness, and the absolute of divine revelation, the Abraham narratives deserve a positive, respectful approach; any other risks destroying any evidence they afford' (Millard 1992: I.40).

[6] E.g., *'Si la foi historique d'Israel n'est pas fondée dans l'histoire, cette foi est erronée, et la notre aussi'* (de Vaux 1965: 7).

acknowledge that the narrative of the folkloric and legendary 'events' ofthe past functions as an honourable medium for the communication of truth, although it is not history in the sense of recording what actuallyhappened. To abandon one's attachment to the historicity of the events of the narrative in the light of compelling contrary evidence is not to forsake belief.

The narrative of the Book of Deuteronomy does not care much for the indigenous population. The notion of the land as the gift of God must reckon with the fact that, invariably, one takes the land from its original inhabitants. The dream of colonisers customarily exacts a nightmare for the indigenous population, and, *pace* Miller (1969: 465) and others, it is not morally acceptable to predicate the land as one's own even 'by the grace of God'. It is some comfort to be rescued from a literalist reading of Deuteronomy, since such a reading predicates a god who shares the predictable dispositions of a ghetto community in an exclusivist, ethnicist, xenophobic and militaristic fashion. While modern biblical scholarship is united in concluding that the narrative of the Pentateuch (the five books of the Bible, Genesis, Exodus, Leviticus, Numbers and Deuteronomy) does not correspond to what actually happened (Whybray 1995: 141), it is not acceptable to allow the narratives to escape an evaluation based on criteria of morality, especially in the light of the use to which they have been put. Subsequent use of the pentateuchal narrative and the so-called deuteronomistic history (Genesis-Kings), especially in the liturgy (formal public worship), invites new generations of hearers/readers to embrace the values of separateness appropriate to (a section of) the Israelite community. One would hope that the generations of participants in the liturgy would be stimulated by these texts rather less energetically than were the Crusaders, the Medieval theologians justifying the conquest of the New World, the Pilgrim Fathers, the South African Calvinists, and, most recently, the more enthusiastic religious Zionists.

A historiography of Israelite origins based solely, or primarily on the biblical narratives is an artificial construct determined by certain religious motivations obtaining at a time long post-dating any verifiable evidence of events. The way forward is to write a comprehensive, independent history of the Near East into which the Israelite history of origins should be fitted. While there is nothing like a scholarly consensus in the array of recent studies on Israel's origins,[7] there is virtual unanimity that the model of tribal conquest as narrated in Joshua 1-12 is untenable (see, e.g., Thompson 1987: 11-40). Leaving aside the witness of the Bible, we have no evidence that there was a Hebrew conquest. Moreover, there is a virtual scholarly consensus that the biblical narratives which describe the conquest-settlement period come from authors writing many centuries later than the 'events' described (whether in the exilic, or post-exilic periods), who had no reliable information about that distant past.

The Exodus-Settlement accounts reflect a particular genre, the goal of which is to inculcate religious values, rather than merely present empirical facts of history. The modern historian must distinguish between the actual history of the peoples and the history of their self-understanding. The archaeology of Palestine must be a primary source for tracing the origins of Israel, and it shows a picture quite different from that of the religiously motivated writings (Ahlström 1993: 28-29). The archaeological evidence points in an altogether different direction from that suggested by Joshua 1-12. It suggests a sequence of periods marked by a gradual and peaceful coalescence of disparate peoples into a group of highland dwellers whose achievement of a new sense of unity culminated only with the entry of the Assyrian administration. The Iron I Age settlements on the central hills of Palestine, from which the later kingdom of Israel developed, reflect continuity with Canaanite culture, and repudiate any ethnic distinction between 'Canaanites' and 'Israelites'. Israel's origins were within Canaan, not outside it. There was neither invasion from outside, nor revolution within. Moreover, the 'Israel' of the period of the biblical

---

[7] In their attempts to construct a history of Israel, Soggin (1984) and Miller and Hayes (1986) mark a departure from the confidence of earlier scholarship in their scepticism concerning the historicity of the biblical traditions of the premonarchic period. They question our ability to say anything sure about Israel's origins, and concur in the judgement that little can be learned from the Bible on the subject, and, in particular, that the traditions of Genesis-2 Kings are of limited use for that purpose. At the level of reception, the societal contexts of modern historians of Israelite origins are reflected in their work. One detects in German historiography of Israel a preoccupation with the nation state after the model of Bismarck's unification of Germany. In American scholarship, the recent history of the 'pilgrim fathers' stressed the model of a chosen people in search of a promised land. In the case of Israeli historiographers, these emphases find an echo in terms of the origins of the modern state of Israel (see Coote and Whitelam 1987: 173-77).

narrative represented a multiplicity of 'ethnic' identities, reflecting the variety of provenances in the Late Bronze-Iron Age transition, and that brought about by three waves of systematic, imperial population transferand admixture (Assyrian, Babylonian and Persian). The predication of Israelite ('ethnic') distinctiveness prior to the Persian period is illusory, and the unity of the biblical 'children of Israel' is a predilection of the biblical authors, rather than the reality reflecting a commonality of ethnic identity or communal experience.

The contemporary needs of the final redactors of the biblical narrative determined and dominated their ideological stance, which we may wish to call religious or pastoral, and issued in an ideal model for the future which they justified on the basis of its retrojection into the past of Israelite origins, the details of which only the surviving conflicting folkloric traditions provided. If we excuse the biblical writers for their misrepresentation of the past on the basis of their paraenetic motives for their own circumstances, we ought not to be equally indulgent with theologians and Church-Synagogue people for whom the evidence of what happened in the past is more reliable. The legendary account of Joshua 1-12 offers no legitimising paradigm for land plunder in the name of God, or by anyone arrogating to himself His authority. Indeed, the extra-biblical evidence promotes a respect for the evolution of human culture, rather than for a process that can deal with adjustment to changed circumstances only by way of violent destruction.

While generations of religious people have derived both profit and pleasure from the retelling of the biblical stories, the victims of the colonialist plunder to whom we have alluded are likely to be less sanguine in their attitude to the texts, and would welcome any attempt to distinguish between the apparent ethnocentricity of the God of Genesis-Kings, and the paraenetic and political intentions of authors writing much later. A major epistemological question arises. Do texts which belong to the genre of folkloric epic or legend, rather than of a history which describes what actually happened, confer legitimacy on the 'Israelite' possession of the land, and on subsequent forms of colonialism, for which the biblical paradigm understood as factual history was appealed to for legitimisation later? Does a judgement which is based on the premise that the genre of the justifying text is history in that sense not dissolve when it is realised that the text belongs to the genre of *myths of origin,* which are encountered in virtually every society, and which were deployed in the service of particular ideologies?

Conclusion

As we have seen, the biblical claim of the divine promise of land is integrally linked with the claim of divine approval for the extermination of the indigenous people. It is assumed widely that its literary genre is history, even though this view runs in the face of all serious scholarly comment. These land traditions pose fundamental moral questions, relating to one's understanding of the nature of God, of His dealings with humankind, and of human behaviour. They have been deployed in support of barbaric behaviour in a wide variety of contexts, for close on two thousand years. The communities which have preserved and promulgated those biblical traditions, then, must shoulder some of the responsibility for what has been done in alleged conformity with the values contained within them.

The behaviour of communities and nation states is complex, and is rarely the result of one element of motivation. Colonialist and imperialist enterprises derive from a matrix of interactive determinants. The colonisation of Latin America in the medieval period had a devastating effect on the indigenous population, the consequences of which perdure to this day. Although it was fuelled by a concurrence of motivations, medieval Christian theocratic imperialism was a major element of its justification. Its ideological underpinning was traced back to biblical paradigms of 'ethnic cleansing' and 'belligerent settler colonialism', the legitimisation of which had the authority of Sacred Scripture.

Although the primary motivation of the Dutch colonisers who trekked from the Cape was economic and social, subsequent ideologues of a fabricated Afrikaner nationalism erected an ideological structure of Christian nationalism which had the biblical paradigm of settler colonialism at its foundation. The pattern of 'separation' and 'separate development' was justified by the prevailing Christian theologians, who traced its moral justification to the alleged behaviour of the Israelites in the pre-conquest and settlement periods. Although *apartheid* became a term which evoked virtually universal opprobrium, it was deployed within an ideological framework which derived from a particular form of Christian nationalism which looked to the biblical paradigm as its ultimate, Godly-assured justification. Although its durability proved to be very limited, *apartheid* wreaked havoc on the indigenous people, leaving South Africa with the greatest recorded inequality of any country of the world

Political Zionism appealed to a range of factors to warrant its form of settler colonialism. Although it was resisted by most religious Jews from the beginning, it was able to exploit, somewhat cynically given the non- and anti-religious dispositions of its proponents, an appeal to God's gift of the land, as narrated in the *Torah-from-Heaven:* Zionism could rest its case on the source of all authority. However, the realisation of the 'Zionist dream' has been an unmitigated nightmare for the population of Palestine.

Although each enactment of the colonial enterprise has its own distinctive qualities, there are common elements by which virtually all colonial endeavours struggle to justify themselves. Invariably these include assertions of superiority over the natives, and the pretence of endowing them with the fruits of a superior order—being 'outposts of progress' in 'the heart of darkness'. In the colonial ventures which emanated out of Europe, the motivation customarily had a strong religious element, and looked to the biblical paradigm for irreproachable authorisation. South African Calvinists have repudiated, and repented for their use of the biblical legend to justify their treatment of the Blacks and Coloureds. The descendants of medieval Spanish and Portuguese colonialists and their victims struggle to repair some of the devastation whose effects perdure.

The situation with respect to Israel-Palestine is unique. The application of a literalist reading of the biblical mandate appears to be more apposite for Jews than for others who appeal to it to justify land occupation. The predicament is particularly poignant in virtue of the Nazi determination to annihilate Jews and Judaism. However, the victims of Auschwitz would hardly approve of a previously oppressed people now oppressing an innocent third party, and exacting as the price of its own liberation the permanent dispossession and servitude of the other: 'The victims of Auschwitz would never have bombed Beirut' (Timerman 1984: 7). There is little indication that Zionism will reverse the spoliation it has caused, or will be checked in its exploitative intentions.

Uniquely in the discourse of colonialist enterprises, Zionists not only protest their innocence, but even while perpetrating the comprehensive oppression of another people they retain the psychology of victims, and even blame the victims. No less uniquely, Zionism has managed to retain the support of much of the West, at least until recently. Instead of engaging in an ongoing critique of Zionism's reduction of the ideals of Judaism to those portions of its tradition which betray a narrow and exclusivist concept of a tribal god, some Christians, especially those involved in the Jewish-Christian dialogue, accept as a compulsory part of the dialogue the obligation to support unconditionally an unrestrained and militant Zionism, as if it were the sole authentic expression of Judaism. Meanwhile, without the critical solidarity of the Western 'Christian' world, whose conscience has been crippled in the wake of the Holocaust, the behaviour of the State of Israel towards the Palestinians has earned widespread international criticism, and is a cause of great distress among many people, including of course many Jews, albeit virtually entirely from the secular camp. *Torah*-driven zealotry is at the forefront of the oppression of the indigenous Palestinians.

Recent scholarship on Israelite origins challenges profoundly many of the 'givens' of the previous discourse. Literary and historical investigation has convinced virtually all scholars that the genre of the patriarchal, pentateuchal and conquest-settlement narratives is not history, but is part of the fabricated myth of origins in the process of 'nation'-building in the wake of the Babylonian exile, and perhaps later in the Persian period. In that light, it is injudicious to conclude that God made the promise of progeny and land to Abraham after the fashion indicated in Genesis 15, and that the occupation took place as described in Joshua 1-12. No critical biblical scholar regards the account in Joshua as reflecting what actually happened prior to the establishment of the Israelites as a 'national' group. The archaeological evidence suggests a sequence of periods marked by a gradual and peaceful coalescence of disparate peoples into a group whose achievement of a new sense of unity culminated only with the entry of the Assyrian administration. The biblical narratives are literary compositions which refract the unknown details of an unrecoverable historical past, and serve them up in a series of legends, epics and myths of 'national' origins, which are deployed in a new social, political, and particularly religious context. The authors of these compositions, which, at a minimum, come from a period of not less than five hundred years after the 'events' had no intention of using them as justification for the extermination of 'Others'.

Moreover, notions of a strictly linear ethnic descent from (a legendary) Abraham to today's Jewish emigrants to Israel are illusory. Historical sources do not allow us to differentiate between 'Israelites' and 'Canaanites', and they point to Israelite origins within the land, rather than outside it as the biblical narrative insists. Moreover, the variety of people in Palestine at the time of the so-called Israelite settlement, and later included within the 'people of Israel' during the creation of the regional kingdoms of Israel and Judah, coupled with the effects of the population transfer and replacement of the Assyrian, Babylonian and Persian empires preclude the common assumption that one is dealing with a homogeneous 'people of Israel', ethnically, culturally and religiously one at all periods.

The presumption that the biblical paradigm of land-possession portrayed at one period has an automatic currency for quite a different one, whether in medieval Latin America, or nineteenth-twentieth century Afrikaner and Zionist nationalism is not sustainable. Moreover, it is not without irony that the Bible, and its use as a legitimating document for the colonial ventures we have discussed, is applied against the interests of peoples for whom the biblical text had no corresponding authority. The very application by outsiders, Christian and Jewish, of the world-view of the Bible to a people for whom it had no authoritative standing, is a striking example of religious and political imperialism.[8]

Against the background of even some knowledge of the consequences of colonisation for indigenous populations, biblical scholarship has been modest in its concern for the moral dimension of the problematic. Since virtually all of the scholarship has been done since the establishment of the State of Israel in 1948, and most of it since 1967, the achievement of biblical scholarship, when judged by its concern for the indigenous people, and the values enshrined in

---

[8] The pre-colonial inhabitants of southern Africa were not literate, and the peoples of Latin America had their own highly sophisticated systems of religion. In 1914 Palestine, three years before the British conquest, the population of the area was 757,182, with 590,890 (78 per cent) Muslim, 83,794 (11 per cent) Jewish, and 73,024 (9.6 per cent) Christian (Abu-Lughod 1987: 142). Today, 98 per cent of the Palestinian population within the areas controlled by Israel are Muslims, for whom the biblical text, in the strict sense, is outside their religious and cultural framework.

international law and conventions on human rights, is not impressive. The support which these activities have acquired from theological and exegetical assertions from within academic and religious circles, Jewish and Christian, is not a legacy which I am proud to bequeath to the next generation of exegetes and religious. Such support in my generation will elicit condemnation and repudiation from future generations, in a manner corresponding to the way other forms of theocratic colonialisms have been rejected. Ultimately, and probably soon, other traditions within Judaism and Christianity will achieve enough support to ensure that Judaism will not be condemned forever to those forms of theocratic imperialism which receive support from only the more disreputable traditions of the Bible, and from those forms of Jewish and Christian eschatology which are scandalous to even secular humankind.

The ongoing identification in subsequent history with the warring scenes of the Hebrew Bible is a burden the biblical tradition must bear. The fact that the particular violence of the Hebrew Scriptures has inspired violence, and has served as a model of, and for persecution, subjugation, and extermination for millennia beyond its own reality makes investigation of these biblical traditions a critical and important task (see Niditch 1993: 4). Nevertheless, the ethnocentric, xenophobic and militaristic character of the biblical fabricated myth of origins is treated in conventional biblical scholarship as if it were above any questioning on moral grounds, even by criteria derived from other parts of the Bible. Most commentators are uninfluenced by considerations of human rights, when these conflict with a naive reading of the sacred text, and appear to be unperturbed by its advocacy of plunder, murder, and the exploitation of indigenous peoples, all under the guise of fidelity to the eternal validity of the Sinaitic covenant (see Prior 1997: 253-86).

This is especially true of the seminal studies of W D Davies, the most significant in the field. His 1974 study was written at the request of friends in Jerusalem, who just before the war in 1967, urged his support for the cause of Israel (1982: xiii). His second work was written under the direct impact of that war: 'Here I have concentrated on what in my judgement must be the beginning for an understanding of this conflict: the sympathetic attempt to comprehend the Jewish tradition' (1982: xiii-xiv). Its updated version was written because of the mounting need to understand its theme in the light of events in the Middle East, culminating in the Gulf War and its aftermath (1991: xiii).

While Davies considers the topic from virtually every conceivable perspective in his 1974 and 1982 works, little attention is given to broadly moral and human rights' issues. Davies takes the establishment of the pre-1967 Jewish State of Israel in his stride. Only the post-1967 occupation is a problem. The colonial plunder associated with the foundation of the State of Israel is above reproach, and appears to enjoy the same allegedly divinely sanctioned legitimacy and mandate as the Joshua-led encroachment on the land.

Davies excluded from his concern, 'What happens when the understanding of the Promised Land in Judaism conflicts with the claims of the traditions and occupancy of its other peoples'. He excuses himself by saying that to engage that issue would demand another volume (1991: xv), without indicating his intention to embark upon such an enterprise. Similarly, at the end of his 1981 article (p. 96), he claimed that it was impossible to discuss that issue. One wonders whether Davies would be equally sanguine had white, Anglo-Saxon Protestants, or even white Catholics of European provenance been among the displaced people who paid the price for the enactment of the divine mandate. He shows no concern for the fundamental injustice done to the Palestinian Arabs by the encroachment on their land by Zionists, and for the compensation that justice and morality demands. Despite the foundational plunder of 1948, Davies writes as if there were now a moral equivalence between the dispossessed Palestinians and the dispossessor Zionists. The rights of the victim and the rapist are finely balanced.

For his part, the esteemed American archaeologist William Foxwell Albright had no qualms of conscience about the plunder attendant upon Joshua's enterprise, which was understood by Albright in a largely historically reliable way:

> From the impartial standpoint of a philosopher of history, it often seems necessary that a people of markedly inferior type should vanish before a people of superior potentialities, since there is a point beyond which racial mixture cannot go without disaster ... It was fortunate for the future of monotheism that the Israelites of the Conquest were a wild folk, endowed with primitive energy and ruthless will to exist, since the resulting decimation of the Canaanites prevented the complete fusion of the two

> kindred folk which would almost inevitably have depressed Yahwistic standards to a point where recovery was impossible. Thus the Canaanites, with their orgiastic nature worship, their cult of fertility in the form of serpent symbols and sensuous nudity, and their gross mythology, were replaced by Israel, with its pastoral simplicity and purity of life, its lofty monotheism, and its severe code of ethics. In a not altogether dissimilar way, a millennium later, the … Carthaginians with the gross Phoenician mythology … with human sacrifices and the cult of sex, were crushed by the immensely superior Romans, whose stern code of morals and singularly elevated paganism remind us in many ways of early Israel (Albright 1957: 280-81).

Whitelam sees in this account an outpouring of undisguised racism, which stands in a long line of Orientalist representations of the Other as the opposite of the Western, rational intellectual:

> Even after sixteen years, well after the full horrors of the Holocaust had been exposed, Albright felt no need to revise his opinion that 'superior' peoples had the right to exterminate 'inferior'. Nor did he acknowledge the startling paradox of his theology which fails to recognize the offensiveness of the idea that Israelite monotheism was saved in its 'lofty ethical monotheism' by the extermination of the indigenous population (Whitelam 1996: 84).

Whitelam is particularly upset that Albright's racist philosophy of history has never received the critique it deserves: either it was too delicate a question, or scholarship colluded in the enterprise (1996: 88). Ironically, it is the archaeological data which have undermined Albright's invention of the past. Whitelam draws attention to Albright's support for Zionism, initially only cultural Zionism, but in the light of 'the monstrous reality of Hitlerism' of political Zionism also: Jews would bring to the Near East all the benefits of European civilisation (Albright 1942). In Whitelam's judgement, Albright's Israel of the Iron Age is a mirror image of the Israel of his time (1996: 90).

Meanwhile, a God who insists on the destruction of people as an act of devotion to Him is one from whom most decent people should recoil. The biblical doctrines of God's Chosen People and Promised Land assume a problematic character when viewed against the colonialist exploitation of them leading to the exspoliation of the indigenous peoples of Latin America, the humiliation of non-whites in South Africa, and, in our own day, to militaristic and xenophobic Zionism, which undermines the integrity of Judaism, embarrasses and shocks most moral people, and wreaks havoc on an innocent third-party. Christians have long abandoned circumcision, the killing of adulterers, and other details of the *Torah* as essential expressions of fidelity to the progressive revelation of God.

'There is no document of civilisation which is not at the same time a document of barbarism' (Benjamin 1973: 258). Biblical scholars have the most serious obligation to prevent outrages being perpetrated in the name of fidelity to the biblical covenant. The application of the Bible in defence of the Crusades, Spanish and Portuguese colonialism, South African apartheid, and political Zionism has been a calamity, leading to the suffering and humiliation of millions of people, and to the loss of respect for the Bible as having something significant to contribute to humanity. Christians caught up in an uncritical approach to the Old Testament may seek refuge in the claim that the problem lies with the predispositions of the modern reader, rather than with the text itself. *Pace* Deist (1994: 28-29) and others, one cannot escape so easily. One must acknowledge that much of the *Torah,* and the Book of Deuteronomy in particular, contains menacing ideologies and racist, xenophobic and militaristic tendencies, and is dangerous when read without respect for its literary genre, and the circumstances of its composition.[9] The moral problem stems from the nature of some of the material of the Bible itself. As Niditch has shown, there is a variety of war traditions in the Bible—she discusses seven—which involve overlap and self-contradiction (1993: 154). The implications of the

---

[9] *Pace* President Clinton, on the night before the White House signing of the Declaration of Principles (13 September 1993), the Book of Joshua is not the best distraction for a person transfixed between wakefulness and sleep. Neither, *pace* Baruch Goldstein, should the Book of Esther be accorded a favoured place in the search for moral exhortation. Hotel managers may need to censor their Gideon Bibles, lest their clients be driven to appalling behaviour in the wake of sleepless nights spent reading some of the more racist, xenophobic and militaristic traditions within the biblical text.

existence of dubious moral dispositions, presented as mandated by the divinity within a book which is canonised as Sacred Scripture, invites the most serious investigation.

However, a solution to the historical problem of Israelite origins does not eliminate the problem posed by the literary narrative. It is the narrative itself, rather than the sophisticated exegesis of it, which hasfuelled colonial adventures. While early Israelite history belongs to the unrecoverable past, the biblical narrative perdures as an instrument of oppression. In the narrative, the entry into a land already occupied by others, followed by not only the warrant to violate the rights of the indigenes, but by the divine mandate to do so, becomes the climax of the liberation to be celebrated. What the narrative requires would be designated war-crimes and crimes against humanity according to modern secular standards of human and political rights. While the results of literary and archaeological investigation of the biblical narrative of Israelite origins, even at this stage, might be very welcome to the Amerindians, the southern African blacks, and the Palestinians, they would be judged to have come rather too late on the scene.

However, while the investigation of the nature and period of composition of the biblical narrative is illuminating in its own right, it is the finished composition which has been accorded canonical status, reflecting its divine provenance. The biblical text has been accorded a position of foundational significance, whether in the Synagogue or the Church, and even, by extension, in the lecture-hall and the 'market-place'. The Bible has enjoyed, and retains a level of authority in much of the globe which is matched only by the Sacred Scriptures of other traditions. The divine provenance accorded it in all its parts, whether by the claim that it comes from heaven (*Torah min-haShamayim*), or as the Word of God (*Dei Verbum*), raises significant moral problems, which I have addressed here. In confronting those traditions which appear to conflict with either one's own humane values, or which appear to contradict a whole range of other traditions, including many within the biblical text itself, one is engaged in a hermeneutical activity of considerable sophistication.

For much of the period of Christendom, Christian theology—of which the study of the Bible is the soul—has enjoyed the status of 'queen of the sciences'. Increasingly since the Enlightenment and the scientific revolution, it has had to settle for a somewhat eccentric position on the periphery of Western culture, and now aspires to acquire a more modest position within the complex of human discourse. Precisely because of the tragedies which have shocked civilisation in this century (two great wars, a list of partially completed genocides, wide availability of weaponry of awesome powers of destruction, etc.), there is wide agreement on questions of human rights, and a sensitivity to the need to curtail the excesses of belligerence. Although many of the conventions are respected more convincingly at the level of rhetoric rather than in practice, they serve as benchmarks against which to measure moral behaviour. By such standards, the biblical traditions we have examined here fall embarrassingly short.

While the scholastic community has provided 'rich and suggestive studies on the "land theme" in the Bible ... they characteristically stop before they get to the hard part, contemporary issues of land in the Holy Land' (Walter Brueggemann, in March 1994: vii). The preferred mode for dealing with the embarrassing traditions of the Bible in one major Christian tradition is by a combination of evasion of the offending traditions (i.e., excluding them altogether from the lectionary and the *Divine Office*), and, where such texts contain edifying elements, of excising from the public liturgy those portions of the Word of God which would perplex worshippers sensitive to the ideals of human rights and international legality (Prior 1997: 273-78). Christian theology and the Christian Church should confront the moral questions which I have considered here. The problem is no less acute for Jewish theology and Judaism.[10] This study is an exploration into terrain virtually devoid of enquirers, and an attempt to map out some of the contours of that terrain. It does not pretend to have all the answers, but it does reflect the author's dissatisfaction with the prevailing scholastic assessments of the matter, especially the most common ones, which prefer the security of silence to risking the opprobrium of speaking out.

The study has moved beyond the conventional exegetical approaches, and attempts to subject the biblical narrative to a *moral-literary analysis*. Rather than provide an exegesis which removes itself from the social, political and moral context, it responds to Erich

---

[10] I regret that my purely general knowledge of Islam does not equip me to comment authoritatively on the relevant Islamic traditions concerning God's gift of land, the exodus, and those traditions which deal with divinely sanctioned violence. Perhaps my attempts to deal with the question from the context of a Christian from the West may encourage Islamic scholars to subject their traditions also to a corresponding moral critique.

Auerbach's appeal to reunify the secular and the religious critical tradition, a task he undertook so tellingly in his *Mimesis* (1946, ET 1953). This study on the link between the Bible and colonialism is a work of applied biblical exegesis which is distinctive in its concern for morality and acceptable human behaviour. It is not simply a protest at the neglect of the moral question in Euro-American biblical hermeneutics, but is also an attempt to rescue the Bible from being a blunt instrument in the oppression of people.

I trust that my conscientious probings into a web of immensely complicated issues, within and between conventionally disparate discourses, will encourage others to attempt to deal with the substantial issues I raise. I hope that my work contributes to a rise in moral indignation at what has been perpetrated on indigenous peoples by colonisers, with the support of the biblical paradigm of alleged settler colonisation at the behest of the divinity. It is my hope that my enterprise will promote a discourse that questions present assumptions. It invites comment on the 'value of our values', and in particular on the problematic of the bloodshed that was justified by the piety of the 'good'. My study has a diagnostic function. It uncovers layers below the surface, and names them. The intent is not only diagnostic, however, but aspires also to being recuperative, since I contend that the biblical texts have a specific value, and should not be deployed in ways which offend the basic, decent values of a culture most of us hope to create. Future discussion will need to provide a more credible notion of the Bible as the Word of God, of Divine Inspiration, and of the Authority of Sacred Scripture. For no other reason, then, a scholar of the Bible must not be satisfied with an unearthing of the past, but must enquire into its significance and place in contemporary society.

> They were conquerors, and for that you want only brute force—nothing to boast of, when you have it, since your strength is just an accident arising from the weakness of others. They grabbed what they could get for the sake of what was to be got. It was just robbery with violence, aggravated murder on a great scale, and men going at it blind—as is very proper for those who tackle a darkness. The conquest of the earth, which mostly means the taking it away from those who have a different complexion or slightly flatter noses than ourselves, is not a pretty thing

when you look into it too much. What redeems it is the idea only. An idea at the back of it; not a sentimental pretence but an idea; and an unselfish belief in the idea—something you can set up, and bow down before, and offer a sacrifice to (Marlow, in Joseph Conrad's *Heart of Darkness*).

Biblical scholarship must set its own house in order by articulating ethical criteria by which dispositions unworthy of a civilised person may not be accorded a privileged place as part of a sacred text. When the sacred pages are manipulated by forces of oppression, biblical scholars cannot continue to seek refuge by expending virtually all their intellectual energies on an unrecoverable past, thereby releasing themselves from the obligation of engaging in contemporary discourse. Nor are they justified in maintaining an academic detachment from significant engagement in real, contemporary issues. While it may be conceded by some that 'social and political action is not the direct task of the exegete' (Pontifical Biblical Commission 1993: 68), I can think of no circumstance in which such activity is not incumbent on a Christian exegete, as a Christian.

4

THE RIGHT OF RETURN OF DISPLACED JERUSALEMITES

John Quigley

In the negotiations that are to take place between Israel and the Palestine Liberation Organisation (PLO) over the status of Jerusalem, principal attention will focus on the questions of sovereignty and administration. However, the question of the fate of those Palestine Arabs who have been displaced from Jerusalem is important also.

The question of displaced Palestine Arabs is, of course, a separate issue that Israel and the PLO are supposed to address in their so-called 'final status' negotiations. But in resolving the question of the status of Jerusalem, the question of return of displaced Arabs is quite relevant. If displaced Arabs were to return, the city's population balance would be affected, and this in turn would have implications for administration and control.

The Israel-PLO negotiations, according to the Declaration of Principles signed by the two parties in 1993, are to be conducted on the basis of United Nations Security Council Resolution 242, which calls for 'just settlement' of the question of Palestine Arabs who have been displaced. These persons are referred to in the United Nations Security Council's Resolution 242 of 1967 as 'refugees', but this term is inexact in this context. In international practice, the term 'refugee' refers to a person who seeks the right to reside in a foreign country because he does not want to reside in his own country for fear of persecution. Thus, the United Nations convention on refugees, for example, defines 'refugee' in this way.

The Palestine Arabs, however, seek to return to their own country. Thus, they do not fit the definition of 'refugee'. It is more accurate to refer to them as displaced persons, that is, persons who, for reasons not of their own choosing, are living outside their own country. Such persons have, under international law, a right of return. This right is based on the attachment of the person to the person's native territory. That attachment is given recognition in the law. Take, for example, a group of persons who flee a natural disaster, such as a flood, and in order to escape the flood they cross an international border. Once the waters have receded and it is safe for them to return to their country, they have a legal right to do so. If the government of their country decides, for any reason, not to re-admit them, it would be acting unlawfully.

The right of such persons to return is based on two separate bodies of law. The first body of law is the law relating to nationality. A country must allow its nationals to reside in the country's territory. But a country in which aliens are sojourning has no obligation to permit them to reside permanently in its territory. In international practice, each state controls admission of persons to its territory and controls, in particular, the question of which persons shall have residency rights. Thus, if the person's own country refuses to re-admit him, the rights of the other country are violated. The other country has a right to demand that the person be re-admitted.

The second body of law is the law of human rights. Under international law, rights are held not only by countries. They are held as well by individual persons. One of the rights held by persons is the right to reside in their own country. Thus, if a country refuses to re-admit one of its nationals, it violates the rights of that national. This right is found, in particular, in the International Covenant on Civil and Political Rights (article 12), which states that 'no one shall be arbitrarily deprived of the right to enter his own country.' The Universal Declaration of Human Rights, which was adopted by the United Nations General Assembly in 1948, states (article 13) that everyone has a right 'to return to his country'.

This right is found as well in regional treaties on human rights. In three regions of the world—Europe, Africa, and the Americas—a treaty has been concluded to enforce the protection of human rights. In all three of these treaties, the right of return is guaranteed. The European Convention for the Protection of Human Rights and Fundamental Freedoms (Protocol No. 4, article 3) states that 'no one shall be deprived of the right to enter the territory of the state of which he is a national.' The African Charter on Human and Peoples' Rights states (article 12) that 'every individual' is entitled 'to return to his country.' The American Convention on Human Rights states (article 22) that 'no one can be expelled from the territory of the state of which he is a national or be deprived of the right to enter it.'

The government of Israel maintains that the displaced Palestine Arabs, including those from Jerusalem, have no right of return, despite these legal propositions. It argues that the country in question is Israel, and that for the displaced Palestine Arabs, Israel is not their country, and in particular that the displaced Palestine Arabs are not nationals of Israel.

As regards displaced Jerusalemites, this argument raises the question of whether Jerusalem is part of Israel. The government of Israel, to be sure, is in control of Jerusalem. In addition, it claims sovereignty in Jerusalem, over both the western and eastern sectors. However, the international community to date has not recognised this claim of sovereignty. As for the eastern sector, the United Nations has strongly condemned Israel's extension of authority there. After the June 1967 war, when Israel occupied eastern Jerusalem, its government decreed that Israeli law and administration would be effective there. The United Nations declared this action to be an annexation, and on this basis found it to be unlawful. The UN Security Council did so in its Resolution 252, and the UN General Assembly did so in its Resolution 2253. Israel held eastern Jerusalem as a belligerent occupant, and under the international law of belligerent occupation, such territory may not be annexed.

Israel had earlier claimed sovereignty over western Jerusalem. In 1950 Israel's Knesset declared the western sector to be Israel's capital, thus claiming sovereignty over it. In 1980 the Knesset decreed that 'Jerusalem, complete and united' was 'the capital of Israel', thus claiming sovereignty over both sectors. This claim of sovereignty was rejected by the United Nations, the Security Council in Resolution 478, and the General Assembly in Resolution 35/169. Governments of other countries have refused to locate their diplomatic missions to Israel in Jerusalem, because they do not view the city (eastern sector or western sector) to be under Israel's sovereignty.

As regards displaced Jerusalemites, Israel argues that they have no right to return because Jerusalem is now Israel's. However, since Israel's claim of sovereignty in Jerusalem is not recognised internationally, this argument is of doubtful validity.

However, even if Israel held sovereignty in Jerusalem, the displaced Jerusalemites would still have a right to return. The attachment of an individual to territory, as protected under international law is such that it is not affected by a change in sovereignty. Let us go back to the example given above of the victims of a flood who flee to another country. If while the flood victims are in the other country their own country is invaded and absorbed by a third country, these persons nonetheless have a right to return. The new sovereign must recognise their rights.

Under international law, this requirement is handled by a rule according to which the residents automatically gain the nationality of a new sovereign, unless they decide not to accept it. This proposition of law was recognised by an Israeli court in which the question arose, shortly after Israel was declared a state. The question arose as to whether Jews who were parties to a lawsuit were nationals of Israel. At the time, Israel had no legislation on nationality. The District court of Tel Aviv ruled that 'in the case of transfer of a portion of the territory of a State to another State, every individual and inhabitant of the ceding state becomes automatically a national of the receiving state'.[1] The court said that if this were not the case, Israel would have had no national prior to its legislation on nationality. It said that 'every individual who, on the date of the establishment of the State of Israel was resident in the territory which today constitutes the State of Israel, is also a national of Israel.'

However, the government of Israel has refused to apply this proposition of law to the displaced Palestine Arabs, including the displaced Jerusalemites. Many Jerusalemites, to be sure, had already been displaced by the time Israel declared itself as a state. This fact,

---

[1] Case of A.B. v. M.B., 6 April, 1951, *International Law Reports 1950*, vol. 17 (1956): 110.

however, does not negate their right to return. Israel is under an obligation to recognise as its nationals all who held Palestine nationality at the time of Israel's formation, even with respect to Palestine nationals who were absent at that time.

Israel has also argued that a return of Palestine Arabs to Jerusalem or elsewhere in territory under its control might undermine its authority or threaten its security. Such considerations are not deemed valid under international law as reasons to deny persons a right to return to their country. However, even if such considerations were valid, they are not relevant in the context of an agreement being negotiated between Israel and the PLO. In such an agreement, the PLO would be recognising that returning Palestine Arabs would be living under whatever territorial arrangement is determined.

The right of return, as here explained, applies even if the government of the territory did not cause the departure of the displaced persons. Thus, in the example given above of the residents who leave because of a flood, the government did not force them to leave. Israel has also given, as a reason to deny return to Palestine Arabs, including Jerusalemites, that they left for reasons of their own, to join armies to oppose Israel, or because Arab leaders instructed them to leave. As the right of return is explained above, however, this question is not relevant to a right of return. Even if the displaced Palestine Arabs left for the reasons indicated by Israel, they would still have a right of return.

In fact, however, those reasons are not accurate. Israel precipitated the departure of most of those who were displaced. Some were forced out by the government of Israel from the walled city in 1967, shortly after Israel came into control. Many more were forced out by violence and the threat of violence in 1948 by the Israel Defence Force and by the Jewish military units that operated in Jerusalem in the early months of 1948. These units committed violent acts designed to intimidate Palestine Arabs out of the western sector of Jerusalem, and their efforts were successful. A population of over 60,000 Palestine Arabs was reduced to only a few thousand. Jerusalemites who were displaced in this fashion have not only a right to return, but a right to compensation for hardships suffered during their departure, and for their inability to reside in their home area for the period of their displacement.

In 1948, Arabs began to flee the western sector of Jerusalem in the early months of the year, as a result of terror tactics aimed against them. In January 1948, the Haganah detonated a bomb in a hotel in an Arab neighbourhood in west Jerusalem, killing 26 persons. The British government called the bombing a 'dastardly and wholesale murder of innocent people' ('Britain Condemns Haganah "Murders"', *New York Times*, 7 January 1948, p. A1). During the same month, the Haganah launched rockets into Arab neighbourhoods in Jerusalem, with the apparent aim of frightening Arab residents into fleeing.

In a speech in February 1948, Jewish Agency leader David Ben Gurion expressed satisfaction over this exodus of Arabs from Jerusalem. He said, 'Since Jerusalem's destruction in the days of the Romans, it hasn't been so Jewish as it is now.' In 'many Arab districts' in west Jerusalem, he said, 'one sees not one Arab. I do not assume that this will change.' The Haganah sent a van with a loudspeaker into Arab neighbourhoods in west Jerusalem, ordering them to leave (Morris 1987: 50-52).

In April 1948, the Irgun and LEHI (Stern Gang) captured the village of Deir Yassin on the western outskirts of Jerusalem, and after suppressing armed resistance killed 250 civilians ('200 Arabs Killed, Stronghold Taken', *New York Times*, 10 April 1948, p. A6). The Irgun drove survivors of the Deir Yassin massacre through the streets of Jerusalem in trucks, in an apparent effort to frighten Jerusalem's Arabs into fleeing. The Haganah operated loudspeaker vans in Jerusalem, announcing in Arabic, 'unless you leave your homes, the fate of Deir Yassin will be your fate.'

Under international law, Israel is responsible for these acts of intimidation. A state is responsible for the acts of its military units, even if the state did not direct the units to act in this illegal way. Thus, Israel is responsible for forcing the exodus of the Arabs of Jerusalem even if there was no overall plan at the leadership level to force them out. It is responsible if acts of intimidation leading to departure were committed by its military units.

Many of the acts of intimidation in question, of course, occurred in the first months of 1948, before Israel existed as a state. Under international law, Israel is responsible for those acts. The rule in international law is that a new state is responsible for acts of insurgent or irregular military forces, where the efforts of those forces result in its creation as a state. Thus, Israel is responsible for acts of intimidation committed by the Haganah, the Irgun, and LEHI.

The government of Israel has rejected the idea of a return by

Palestine Arabs, including Jerusalemites. Its argument has been that this issue cannot be addressed separately from that of an overall settlement between Israel on the one side, and the Palestinians and neighbouring Arab states on the other. Now that such an overall settlement is in process, it has changed the reason for rejecting a return.

Prime Minister Benjamin Netanyahu has said that his government rejects 'the right of return of Arab populations to any part of the Land of Israel west of the Jordan River' ('Netanyahu hits first Crisis over Cabinet Line-up', *Independent* [London], 19 June 1996, p. 10). Netanyahu's rationale for this position, as explained by a government spokesperson, is 'demographic security', by which it means that a return would dilute the Jewish numerical predominance. ('Religious Issues delay Coalition Deal', *Jerusalem Post*, 17 June 1996, p. 1). This rationale has no basis in law and amounts to discrimination on ethnic grounds.

In international conflicts in which displacement of population has occurred, the return of displaced persons is viewed by the United Nations as an essential component of a settlement agreement. The United Nations has taken this position regarding the conflict in Palestine. The General Assembly in its Resolution 194 of 1948 called on Israel to repatriate displaced Palestinians, and the Assembly has repeated this call in even stronger terms in more recent years. The Security Council adopted a resolution in the wake of the 1967 war, Resolution 237, in which it called on Israel to repatriate the Arabs displaced during that conflict.

In conflicts in other parts of the world, the United Nations has taken the same position. With the conflict in Bosnia, the Council said, in Resolution 779 (1992), that 'all displaced persons have the right to return in peace to their former homes,' and in Resolution 787 (1992) 'insist(ed) that all displaced persons be enabled to return in peace to their former homes.' Resolution 876 (1993) on Abkhazia, a territory from which Georgian inhabitants fled during civil warfare, affirmed the right of refugees and displaced persons to return to their homes. With Croatia, from which many Serb inhabitants fled, the Council, in Resolution 1009 (1995), demanded that Croatia 'in conformity with internationally recognized standards ... respect fully the right of the local Serb population including their rights to remain, leave or return in safety ... (and) create conditions conducive to the return of those persons who have left their homes.' The Security Council in these resolutions thus not only calls on the governmental authorities in question to repatriate displaced persons, but indicates that the displaced persons have a right to return, and that the governmental authorities are legally obligated to repatriate them.

The United Nations, unfortunately, is for the moment not taking a central role in the Palestine question. Whereas in the conflicts in the former Yugoslavia and Abkhazia the Security Council is working to get displaced persons back to their home territories, with the displaced Palestinians it is leaving the matter to negotiations between the parties. It is to be hoped that the United Nations will reassert itself and become actively involved in working towards a return of displaced Jerusalemites as part of any agreement regarding the future of Jerusalem.

The recent Security Council's insistence on return of persons displaced in the course of military conflicts is based on the premise that displaced persons are entitled to return, and that if they are not afforded this opportunity, an issue of contention will be left unresolved. Thus, a political agreement that omits return for displaced persons does not resolve all outstanding issues. By leaving a key issue unresolved, such an agreement runs the risk of being an agreement only on paper. Any agreement about the future of Jerusalem must provide for the repatriation of the displaced Jerusalemites. This result is the only wise choice from the political standpoint, and is required by international law.

ADDENDUM

Details of the Jerusalem Day Symposia

All the papers delivered at the other symposia have been published in Arabic and are available from the Jerusalem Day Committee.

The First Symposium (2-5 October 1989)

It was held in Kuwait, under the patronage of HE Abdel Aziz El-Saqer, Chairman of the Chamber of Commerce, Kuwait. After the Opening Ceremonies, the following papers were presented:

Dr Ishaq Ubeid
> Professor of History of the Middle Ages, Ein-Shams University, Cairo
> *The Crusader Invasions were Barbaric Attacks under a Religious Pretext*

Dr Qasem Abdo Qasem

> Associate Professor of History of the Middle Ages, Kuwait University, Kuwait
>
> *The Biblical Elements in the Exploitation of Religion in the Crusader Wars and the Zionist Movement*

Dr Kamel al-'Asali

> History Researcher, University of Jordan, Amman
>
> *Salahuddin Al-Ayyoubi and his Descendants' Institutions in Jerusalem*

Dr Saleh Hamarneh

> Professor of History, University of Jordan, Amman
>
> *Christian Arabs in the Court of Salahuddin Al-Ayyoubi and their Role in opposing the Ifranjah Invasion (Crusaders)*

Dr Fayez Iskander

> Professor of History of the Middle Ages, Benha University, Egypt
>
> *Salahuddin Al-Ayyoubi's Tolerance of Christians during the Liberation Wars of Jerusalem*

Dr Nuriddin Hatoum

> Emeritus Professor of Modern History, Damascus University, University of Kuwait and other Universities
>
> *Arab Unity and its Effect on the Liberation of Jerusalem in the Past and Present*

Dr Khayrieh Qasmyeh

> Professor of Modern History, Damascus University, Damascus
>
> *The Role of Palestinian Women in Resisting foreign Occupation, Crusader, British, and Zionist*

Dr Abdel Jalil-Abdel Mahdi

> Professor of Arab Literature, University of Jordan, Amman
>
> *Jerusalem and the Literature of Resistance during the Crusaders' Invasions*

Dr Shaker Mustafa
> Arab Researcher, Writer, Professor of Islamic History,
> University of Kuwait, Kuwait
> *Salahuddin Al-Ayyoubi's Strategy in the Ramleh Peace Treaty*

Dr Anis Fawzi Qasem
> Editor of *The Palestine Yearbook of International Law*
> *Will the USA move its Embassy to Jerusalem?*

The Proceedings include the Decisions and Recommendations of the Symposium.

The Second Symposium (12-14 October 1991)

It was held in Amman, under the patronage of HE Dr Khaled Al-Karaky, Former Jordanian Minister of Higher Education. After the Opening Ceremonies, the following papers were presented:

Professor Salahuddein Buheiri
> Professor of Geography, University of Jordan, Amman
> *Highlights of the Geopolitics of Jerusalem*

Architect Issam Awwad
> Resident Architect in Charge of Renovating the Dome of the
> Holy Mosque of the Rock, Jerusalem
> *The Dome of the Rock —Its Past and Present.*

Mr Nawwaf El-Zaru
> Journalist and Researcher, Amman
> *Arab Jerusalem in the Context of Judaisation Plans: Palestinian
> Struggle and Solidarity*

Professor Mustafa Hyari
> Professor of History, University of Jordan, Amman
> *Liberation of Jerusalem 1187. A Lesson from the Past on Unity*

Professor Dr Saleh Hamarneh
> Professor of History, University of Jordan, Amman
> *Colonial Imperialist Expansion in the Arab Homeland. A Study of the Zionist Invasion as a Repetition of the Ifranjah (Crusader) Attacks*

Dr Zyad Assali
> Researcher, USA
> *Zionist Studies of the Crusaders' Movements and Wars*

Professor Dr Nicola Zyadeh
> Professor of History in Arab Universities, Historian and Writer
> *The Economic Aspects of the Crusaders' Wars*

Mr Bahjat Abu Gharbyeh
> A distinguished political figure in the history of the Palestinian Struggle
> *The Liberation of Palestine*

The Proceedings include the Decisions and Recommendations of the Symposium.

The Third Symposium (10-13 October 1992)

It was held in Amman, under the patronage of HE Dr Awad Khuleifat, Former Minister of Higher Education. The theme was *Jerusalem: Heritage, Identity and Solidarity.* After the Opening Ceremonies, there was a showing of the documentary film, *The Noble Sanctuary* by Mr Alistair Duncan (Director of the World of Islam Festival Trust, London).

There was an Open Discussion on *Jerusalem: The Cruel Reality and Future Hopes*, moderated by Dr Ahmad Sudki Dajani. The participants were Mr Ibrahim Daqqaq, Dr Albert Aghazarian, Dr Anis F Qasem, Mr Bahjat Abu Gharbyeh, Mr Tareq Masarweh, Sheikh Ekremah Sabri, Mr Abdel Rahman El-Bitar, Mr Ghazi Al-Saadi, Dr Mohammed Adnan El-Bakheet, Dr Musa El-Hussaini, Mrs Muna Shukeir and Mrs Nazek Khalil.

The following papers were presented:

Sheikh Abdel-Aziz El Khayyet
>Former Jordanian Minister for Awqaf and Religious Affairs
>*Muslims and Jerusalem*

His Eminence Bishop George Khader
>Orthodox Bishop of Lebanon
>*Jerusalem in the Consciousness of Christian Arabs*

Mr George Haddad
>Arab Researcher, Writer and Journalist
>*The Role of the Zionist Movement in influencing the Western Churches with particular attention to the Jerusalem Problem*

Dr Kamel al-'Asali
>Researcher, University of Jordan, Amman
>*Jerusalem in Arab and Muslim Heritage*

Dr Islah Jad
>Professor of Sociology, Beir Zeit University, Palestine
>*Women's Role in Jerusalem in supporting the Heritage, Identity and Solidarity of Arab Jerusalemites*

Mr Ibrahim Al-Daqqak
>Researcher
>*The Economic Role of Jerusalem in supporting the Heritage, Identity and Solidarity of Arab Jerusalem*

Mr Walid El-Assali
>Attorney in Jerusalem
>*The Role of Younger Generations in supporting the Heritage, Identity and Solidarity of Arab Jerusalem*

The Proceedings include the Decisions and Recommendations of the Symposium.

The Fourth Symposium (2-5 October 1993)

It was held in Amman, under the patronage of HE Mr Yanal Hikhmat, former Jordanian Minister of Tourism. The theme was *The Monuments of Jerusalem: Towards a Joint Effort to save Them.*

After the Opening Ceremonies, there was a workshop on *The Importance of Monuments in emphasizing the Cultural Aspects of the Nation*, directed by Dr Saleh Hamarneh. The participants were Dr Albert Aghazarian, Dr Hamad Ahmad Abdullah Yousef, Khader Salameh, Dr Raouf Abu Jaber, Dr Shawqui Sha'ath, Mr Issam Awwad, Mr Ali Barakat, and Dr Yousef El-Natsheh.

The following papers were presented:

Dr Beatrice St Laurent
> Researcher, Albright Institute for Archaeological Research, Jerusalem
> *The Restorations of the Dome of the Rock and their Political Significance*

Professor Dr Mehemet Ipserli
> Head of the History Department, School of Arts, Istanbul
> *The Monuments of Jerusalem in the Ottoman Archives*

Dr Marwan Abu Khalaf
> Researcher, Jerusalem University
> *The Distinctive Islamic Character of the City of Jerusalem*

Dr Fawzi Zayadin
> Researcher, Department of Archeology, Jordan
> *The Monuments of Jerusalem from the Byzantine Period until the Salahuddin Al-Ayyoubi Period*

Dr Kamel al-'Asali
> Researcher, University of Jordan, Amman
> *The Dabbaghah Quarter*

Mr Hassan El Karmi
>Researcher and Writer
>*The Sacred Past*

Dr Ghazi Beeshah
>Researcher, Department of Archeology, Jordan*The Holy Sanctuary, the Dome of the Rock in the light of New Excavations and Studies*

Dr Yasmen Zahran
>Head of the Institute of Islamic Archaeology in Al Quds University Jerusalem
>*Facts and Plans for the Institute of Islamic Archaeology in Jerusalem*

The Proceedings include the Decisions and Recommendations of the Symposium.

The Fifth Symposium (9-12 October 1994)

It was held in Amman, under the patronage of HE Taher El Massri, Speaker of the Lower House of Parliament and former Prime Minister. The theme was *Jerusalem, City of Culture and Education.*

After the Opening Ceremonies, there was a workshop on *How to Support the Educational and Cultural Situation in Jerusalem,* directed by Dr Abdel Rahman Yaghie. The participants were Dr Ibrahim Uthman, Dr Ahmad Abu Helal, Dr Ahmad Abu Sheikhah, Miss Ihsan Attyeh, Mr Asa'ad El-Asa'ad, Dr Bahjat Sabri, Dr Jamal Amrue, Dr Assem El-Shehabi, Dr Abdel-Lateef El-Barghouthi.

The following papers were presented:

Mr Hassan El Karmi
>Researcher, Writer
>*Education in Palestine During the Period of the British Mandate*

Dr Adawyeh El Alami
>Former High Rank Official, Ministry of Education
>*Education of Girls in Jerusalem*

Dr Bahjat Sabri
>Professor of History, Najah University, Nablus, Palestine
>*The Role of the Higher Islamic Institute in Religious Education during the British Mandate Period in Palestine*

Dr Kamel al-'Asali
>Researcher, University of Jordan, Amman
>*The Salahuddin Al-Ayyoubi Islamic College in Jerusalem*

Dr Hassan Abdel Kader
>Professor of Geography, University of Jordan, Amman
>*Al-Maqdissi, the Eminent Geographer*

Dr Abdel Aziz El-Labbadi
>Palestinian Red Crescent Association
>*Abu-Abdallah-El-Tamimi, the Jerusalemite Physician*

Dr Saleh Hamarneh
>Professor of History, University of Jordan, Amman
>*Jerusalemite Personality: Dr Ishaq El-Husseini*

Mrs Naimeh Mohammed El-Saleh
>Director of Rawdat El Maaref College, Amman
>*Jerusalemite Personality: Sheikh Mohammed Sulaiman El-Saleh*

The Proceedings include the Decisions and Recommendations of the Symposium.

The Sixth Symposium (2-5 October 1995)

It was held in Amman, under the Patronage of HE Mr Taher El-Masri, Former Prime Minister of Jordan. The theme was *The Arab and Islamic Identity of Jerusalem*.

After the Opening Ceremonies, the following papers were presented:

Professor Dr Kamel Omran
>Professor of Sociology, Damascus University, Damascus
>*The Dangers of the Middle East New Order for the Arab Status of Jerusalem*

Professor Dr Said Abdel Fattah Ashur
>Professor of History, Cairo University, Cairo, Egypt
>Chairman of the Arab Historians' Association
>>*The Mamluks and Jerusalem*

Professor Dr Afif Bahnasi
>Professor of Islamic Art and Architecture, Damascus University, Damascus
>Former Head of the Archeology Department in Syria
>*The Islamic Originality of Jerusalem Monuments and their Decoration*

Dr Mohammed Afifi
>Associate Professor, School of Arts, Cairo University, Cairo
>*The Coptic Presence in Jerusalem up to the Twentieth Century*

Dr Rashad El Imam
>School of Humanities and Sociology, Tunisian University, Tunis
>*Bibliography of the City of Jerusalem*

Mr. Khalil Tufakji
>Head of the Maps Department, Arab Studies Society, Jerusalem
>*A Proposal for the Boundaries of the Capital of Palestine, Jerusalem*

Professor Dr Abdel Wahed Zhannon Taha
>School of Education, Mousel University, Mousel
>*The Scientific Relations between Arab Jerusalem and (the Arabs in) Andalusia*

Mr. Naji Alloush.
>Arab Writer and Researcher
>*Jerusalem in a New Archaeological Study*

The Proceedings include the Decisions and Recommendations of the Symposium.

The Members of The Jerusalem Day Committee
1995-1996

Dr Subhi Ghosheh, MD (Chairman)
Mr Adli Al-Muhtadi
Dr Akram Al-Dajani, MD
Professor Dr Ibrahim Uthman
Mr Mazen Al-Nashashibi
Mr Michael Sindahah
Dr Mousa Al-Husseini, MD
Professor Dr Salah Beheiri
Professor Dr Saleh Hamarneh

Copies of the Proceedings are available from

Jerusalem Day Committee
P.O. Box 940639
Amman 11194
Jordan.
Phone (00 962 6) 691 710 and 607 592
Fax (00 962 6) 607593 and 684260

BIBLIOGRAPHY

Abu Lughod, Janet. 1987. 'The Demographic Transformation of Palestine', in Abu Lughod, Ibrahim, ed. 1987 (2nd ed.). *The Transformation of Palestine. Essays on the Origin and Development of the Arab-Israeli Conflict*. Evanston: Northwestern University Press, pp. 139-63.

Aharoni, Yohanan. 1982. *The Archaeology of the Land of Israel: from the Prehistoric Beginnings to the End of the First Temple Period*. London: SCM.

Ahlström, Goesta W. 1993. *The History of Ancient Palestine from the Palaeolithic Period to Alexander's Conquest*. JSOT SS 146. Sheffield: Sheffield Academic Press.

Albright, William F. 1942. 'Why the Near East needs the Jews', *New Palestine* 32 (9): 12-13.

Albright, William F. 1957. *From the Stone Age to Christianity: Monotheism and the Historical Process*. New York: Doubleday.

Alt, Albrecht. 1925. *Die Landnahme der Israeliten in Palästina: Reformationsprogramm der Universität Leipzig*. Leipzig: University of Leipzig.

_____ 1930. *Die Staatenbildung der Israeliten in Palästina: Reformationsprogramm der Universität Leipzig.* Leipzig: University of Leipzig.

Anati, Emanuel. 1968. *Palestine Before the Hebrews.* Jerusalem: Israel Exploration Society.

Ateek, Naim Stifan. 1991. 'A Palestinian Perspective: The Bible and Liberation', in Sugirtharajah ed. 1991: 280-86.

Auerbach, Erich. 1957. *Mimesis. The Representation of Reality in Western Literature.* New York: Doubleday.

Benjamin, Walter. 1973. 'Theses on the Philosophy of History', in Arendt, Hannah, ed. 1973. *Illuminations.* London: Collins, pp. 253-64.

Bowler, P J. 1989. *The Invention of Progress: The Victorians and the Past.* Oxford: Blackwell.

Brettler, Marc Zvi. 1995. *The Creation of History in Ancient Israel.* London and New York: Routledge.

Brown, Dee. 1981 (orig. 1971). *Bury my Heart at Wounded Knee.* New York: Pocket Books.

Buber, Martin. 1973. *On Zion: The History of an Idea.* New York: Schocken Books.

Buccellati, Giorgio. 1967. *Cities and Nations of Ancient Syria: An Essay on Political Institutions with Special Reference to the Israelite Kingdoms.* Rome: Pontificio Instituto Biblico.

Coote, Robert B and Keith W Whitelam. 1987. *The Emergence of Early Israel in Historical Perspective.* (The Social World of Biblical Antiquity Series, 5). Sheffield: Almond.

Davies, Philip R. 1992. *In Search of 'Ancient Israel'.* JSOTSS 148. Sheffield: Sheffield Academic Press

Davies, W D. 1974. *The Gospel and the Land. Early Christianity and Jewish Territorial Doctrine*. Berkeley: University of California Press.

_____ 1981. 'The Territorial Dimensions of Judaism', in *Intergerini Parietis Septum (Eph. 2:14). Essays Presented to Markus Barth on his Sixty-fifth Birthday*, ed. Hadidian, Dikran Y. Pittsburgh: The Pickwick Press, . 61-96

_____ 1982. *The Territorial Dimensions of Judaism*. Berkeley: University of California Press.

_____ 1985. 'The "Land" in the Pre-Exilic and Early Post-Exilic Prophets', in Butler, J T, E W Conrad, and B C Ollenburger (eds.), *Understanding the Word*. JSOTSS 37. Sheffield: JSOT Press, pp. 247-62.

_____ 1991. *The Territorial Dimensions of Judaism. With a Symposium and Further Reflections*. Minneapolis: Fortress.

De Vaux, Roland. 1965. 'Les Patriarches hébreux et l'histoire', in *Revue Biblique* 72: 5-28.

Deist, F E. 1994. 'The Dangers of Deuteronomy: A Page from the Reception History of the Book', in Martínez, F García, A Hilhorst, J T A G M van Ruiten, and A S van der Woude, eds. 1994. *Studies in Deuteronomy. In Honour of C J Labuschagne on the Occasion of his 65th Birthday*. Leiden/New York/Köln: Brill, pp. 13-29.

Dever, William G. 1995. 'Will the Real Israel Stand Up? Archaeology and Israelite Historiography: Part I', *Bulletin of the American Schools of Oriental Research* 297: 61-80.

_____ forthcoming. 'Revisionist Israel Revisited: A Rejoinder to Niels Peter Lemche', *Currents in Research: Biblical Studies*.

Finkelstein, Israel. 1996. 'The Archaeology of the United Monarchy: An Alternative View', in *Levant* 28: 177-87.

Frazer, Sir J G. 1896. *Psyche's Task: A Discourse Concerning the Influence of Superstition on the Growth of Institutions.* London: Macmillan.

Garbini, Giovanni. 1988. *History and Ideology in Ancient Israel.* London: SCM.

Gottwald, Norman K. 1979. *The Tribes of Yahweh. A Sociology of the Religion of Liberated Israel, 1250-1050 BCE.* London: SCM.

Gould, Stephen Jay. 1984. *The Mismeasure of Man.* Harmondsworth: Penguin.

Grabbe, Lester, ed. 1997. *Is a History of Israel Possible?* Sheffield: Sheffield Academic Press.

Gray, John. 1969. *A History of Jerusalem.* London: Hale.

Halpern, Baruch. 1995. 'Erasing History: The Minimalists Assault on Ancient Israel', *Bible Review*, December, pp. 26-35, 47.

Hourani, Albert. 1980. *Europe and the Middle East.* Berkeley: University of California Press.

Jamieson-Drake, D W. 1991. *Scribes and Schools in Monarchic Judah. A Socio-archaeological Approach.* Sheffield: Almond Press.

Kedourie, Elie. 1978. *England and the Middle East: the Destruction of the Ottoman Empire, 1914-1921.* Hassocks: Harvester Press.

Khalidi, Walid. 1996. *Islam, the West and Jerusalem.* London: Hood Books.

Lehn, Walter (in association with Uri Davis). 1988. *The Jewish National Fund.* London and New York: Kegan Paul International.

Lemche, Niels Peter. 1985. *Early Israel: Anthropological and Historical Studies on the Israelite Society before the Monarchy.* Vetus Testamentum Supplements 38. Leiden: Brill.

_____ 1988. *Ancient Israel: A New History of Israelite Society*. Leiden: Brill.

_____ 1991. *The Canaanites and their Land: The Tradition of the Canaanites*. Sheffield: JSOT Press.

_____ 1995. (Reprint of original 1988.) *Ancient Israel. A New History of Israelite Society.* The Biblical Seminar 5. Sheffield: Sheffield Academic Press.

Lohfink, Norbert. 1996. 'The Laws of Deuteronomy. Project for a World without any Poor', in *Scripture Bulletin* 26: 2-19.

March, W Eugene. 1994. *Israel and the Politics of Land. A Theological Case Study* (Foreword by Walter Brueggemann). Louisville: Westminster/John Knox Press.

Mazar, Amihai. 1994. 'Jerusalem and Its Vicinity in the Iron Age I', in *From Nomadism to Monarchy: Archaeological and Historical Aspects of Early Israel*, ed. I Finkelstein and N Na'aman. Jerusalem: Israel Exploration Society: 70-91.

Melman, B. 1992. *The Invention of Progress: the Victorians and the Past*. Oxford: Blackwell.

Mendenhall, George E. 1962. 'The Hebrew Conquest of Palestine' in *Biblical Archaeologist* 25: 66-87.

Millard, A R. 1992. 'Abraham', in *The Anchor Bible Dictionary,* Vol 1 (A-C) I.35-41.

Miller, Patrick D, Jr. 1969. 'The Gift of God. The Deuteronomic Theology of the Land', in *Interpretation* 23: 451-67.

Miller, J Maxwell and John H Hayes. 1986. *A History of Ancient Israel and Judah*. Philadelphia: Westminster/London: SCM.

Mofokeng, Takatso A. 1988. *Black Christians, the Bible and Liberation. Journal of Black Theology* 2.

Morris, Benny. 1987. *The Birth of the Palestinian Refugee Problem, 1947-1949*. Cambridge: Cambridge University Press.

————— 1995. 'Falsifying the Record. A Fresh Look at Zionist Documentation of 1948', in *Journal of Palestine Studies* 24: 44-62.

Moscati, Sabatino. 1967. *The Origin of the Semites*. Rome: Pontificio Instituto Biblico.

Neher, André. 1992. 'The Land as Locus of the Sacred', in Burrell, David and Y Landau. 1992. *Voices from Jerusalem. Jews and Christians Reflect on the Holy Land*. New York: Paulist, pp. 18-29.

Neusner, Jacob. 1990. 'The Role of History in Judaism: The Initial Definition', in Neusner, Jacob, ed. 1990. *The Christian and Judaic Invention of History*. Atlanta: Scholars Press, pp. 233-48.

Newman, David, ed. 1985. *The Impact of Gush Emunim. Political Settlement in the West Bank*. London and Sydney: Crook Helm.

Niditch, Susan. 1993. *War in the Hebrew Bible. A Study of the Ethics of Violence*. Oxford: Oxford University Press.

Niemann, H M. 1993. *Herrschaft, Königtum und Staat: Skizzen zur soziokulturelle Entwicklung im monarchischen Israel*. Tübingen: Mohr.

Peters, F E. 1996. 'The Holy Places', in *City of the Great King: Jerusalem from David to the Present*, ed. Nitzka Rosovsky. Cambridge, Mass: Harvard University Press, pp. 37-59.

Pontifical Biblical Commission. 1993. *The Interpretation of the Bible in the Church*. Boston: St Paul Books and Media.

Prior, Michael. 1994. 'Clinton's Bible, Goldstein's Hermeneutics', in *Middle East International* 16 December: 20-21.

_____ 1997. *The Bible and Colonialism. A Moral Critique*. The Biblical Seminar 48. Sheffield: Sheffield Academic Press.

Provan, Iain W. 1995. 'Ideologies, Literary and Critical: Reflections on Recent Writing on the History of Israel', *Journal of Biblical Literature* 141: 585-606.

Rainey, Anson. 1995. 'Review of Th.L. Thompson, *Early History of the Israelite People*', *American Jewish Studies* 20: 156-60.

Said, Edward W. 1988. 'Michael Walzer's *Exodus and Revolution*: A Canaanite Reading', in Said, Edward W and Christopher Hitchens, ed. 1988. *Blaming the Victims. Spurious Scholarship and the Palestinian Question*. London/New York: Verso, pp. 161-78.

_____ 1992. *The Question of Palestine*, London: Vintage.

Schürer, E. 1979. *The History of the Jewish People in the Age of Jesus Christ (175 BC-AD 135)*, vol. II, revised and ed. by G Vermes, *et al.* Edinburgh: T and T Clark.

Seward, Desmond. 1995. *The Monks of War. The Military Religious Orders*. London: Penguin Books.

Shiblak, Abbas. 1986. *The Lure of Zion. The Case of the Iraqi Jews*. London: Al Saqi Books.

Sjeggestad, Marit. 1993. '"Israels tidlige historie"—senere og senere ? En vurdering av Th. L. Thompsons siste bok', *Norsk Teologisk Tidsskrift* 94: 97-108.

Smith, George Adam. 1894. *The Historical Geography of the Holy Land especially in relation to the History of Israel and of the Early Church*. London: Hodder and Stoughton.

Soggin, J Alberto. 1984. *A History of Israel. From the Beginnings to the Bar Kochba Revolt, AD 135*. London: SCM.

Sugirtharajah, R S. ed. 1991. *Voices from the Margin: Interpreting the Bible in the Third World.* London: SPCK.

Tamarin, Georges R. 1973 (ed. Johan Niezing). *The Israeli Dilemma. Essays on a Warfare State.* Rotterdam: Rotterdam University Press.

Thompson, Thomas L. 1974. *The Historicity of the Pentateuchal Narratives. The Quest for the Historical Abraham.* Berlin/New York: de Gruyter.

———— 1979. *The Settlement of Palestine in the Bronze Age*, Beihefte zur Tübinger Atlas des vorderen Orients 34. Wiesbaden: Dr Reichert.

———— 1987. *The Origin Tradition of Ancient Israel. 1. The Literary Formation of Genesis and Exodus 1-23.* JSOTSS 55. Sheffield: JSOT Press.

———— 1992. *Early History of the Israelite People from the Written and Archaeological Sources*, Studies in the History of the Ancient Near East, 4. Leiden: Brill.

———— 1992a. 'Palestinian Pastoralism and Israel's Origins', in *Scandanavian Journal of the Old Testament* 6: 1-13.

———— 1995. 'House of David, an Eponymic Referent to Yahweh as Godfather', in *Scandanavian Journal of the Old Testament* 9: 62-65.

Thompson, Thomas L, F J Gonçalves and J M van Cangh. 1988. *Toponymie Palestinienne. Plaine de St Jean D'Acre et Corridor de Jérusalem.* Louvain-la-Neuve: Université Catholique de Louvain, *Publications de l'Institut Orientaliste de Louvain* (no. 37).

Timerman, Jacobo. 1984. *The Longest War. Israel in Lebanon.* New York: Simon and Schuster.

Van Seters, John. 1975. *Abraham in History and Tradition*. New Haven/London: Yale University Press.

Wright, George E. 1950. *The Old Testament against its Environment*. London: SCM

Warrior, Robert Allen. 1991. 'A North American Perspective: Canaanites, Cowboys, and Indians', in Sugirtharajah, ed. 1991: 287-95.

Whitelam, Keith W. 1996. *The Invention of Ancient Israel: The Silencing of Palestinian History*. London and New York: Routledge.

Whybray, R Norman. 1995. *Introduction to the Pentateuch*. Grand Rapids: Eerdmans.